MADE IN SWINDON

The original settlement came to be known as Old Town after 1841 as New Swindon expanded alongside it. These were merged in 1900 to form a single municipal borough, with the motto Salubritas et Industria. *Translated then as Health and Industry, these might now be called Wellbeing and Work.*

Made in Swindon

A SOCIAL HISTORY 1840s-1940s

EDITED BY

Philip Garrahan

THE HOBNOB PRESS

First published in the United Kingdom in 2025

by The Hobnob Press,
8 Lock Warehouse, Severn Road, Gloucester GL1 2GA
www.hobnobpress.co.uk

© Philip Garrahan and contributors 2025

Philip Garrahan and contributors hereby asserts their moral rights to be identified as the authors of the Work.

All rights reserved. No part of this publication may be reproduced, stored in a retrieval system, or transmitted in any form or by any means, electronic, mechanical, photocopying, recording or otherwise, without the prior permission of the publisher and copyright holder.

British Library Cataloguing in Publication Data
A catalogue record for this book is available from the British Library

ISBN 978-1-914407-88-8

Typeset in Adobe Garamond Pro 11/14 pt.
Typesetting and origination by John Chandler

All royalties accruing from this book will go to Swindon Heritage Preservation Trust (formerly the Mechanics' Institute Trust). The book is published under the copyright fair use exception, as there is no commercial gain. Nevertheless, every effort has been made to contact copyright holders.

Cover illustration: Workmen by Harold Dearden c.1930s. Oil on canvas. 20 x 22.5 cm. In a private collection.

CONTENTS

The Contributors
Acknowledgements

1 Introduction *by* Philip Garrahan   1
2 The Architectural Legacy of Swindon Railway Village
   by Harry Lewis   93
3 The Medical Fund Society 1847-1948 – healthcare from
   cradle to grave before the NHS *by* Adam Busby   33
4 The Mechanics' Institute *by* John Stooke   53
5 Alfred Williams and the Spirit of Swindon *by* Graham Carter   71
6 The Swindon School of Art: picking up steam
   by Philip Dearden   93
7 The Worker As Artist: creativity in a company town
   by Philip Garrahan   117
8 Conclusion: Nostalgia for the Age of Steam *by* Philip Garrahan   145

Delving Deeper   157
Index   161

THE CONTRIBUTORS

THE AUTHORS HAVE extensive experience researching and writing local history. The book has been written to appeal to an informed readership interested in company towns like Swindon. It will also be of value to a wider audience and especially for educational courses in social history.

Adam Busby grew up in Swindon and graduated from Oxford University with a BA in History. His undergraduate dissertation was on the GWR Medical Fund Society. Adam is now a civil servant and maintains a keen interest in historical research.

Graham Carter is a retired journalist and proud to be a born-and-bred Swindonian. He is a co-founder and Vice-Chair of the Alfred Williams Heritage Society and a co-founder and then editor of the quarterly magazine, Swindon Heritage. In 2018 he co-wrote and edited the award-winning A Swindon Time Capsule, a book about the Dixon-Attwell Collection in Swindon Central Library. He has co-written several books with Noel Ponting, most recently a history of The Association of Wiltshiremen in London, called Moonies, Movers and Shakers.

Philip Dearden led the Centre for International Development and Training at the University of Wolverhampton for twenty-five years. He spent seven years in the University as a Professor of International Development and was Associate Dean leading the Research and Knowledge Exchange. Philip is now working as an independent international development consultant and is enjoying researching his grandfather's life and artwork.

Philip Garrahan is a social scientist who taught in four English universities after his doctorate at Reading. His research was in voting behaviour and local political economy and he promoted widening participation to make higher education more inclusive. He was Pro Vice-Chancellor at Sheffield Hallam

University for nine years before retiring in 2010 as Emeritus Professor. He is researching the contribution of art to social history.

Harry Lewis is a proud Swindonian with a family history intertwined with the fortunes of the Works. His background is in architectural history, having received his MA from UCL's Bartlett School of Architecture. He currently works as a built environment consultant that helps developers to navigate the complexities of historic buildings, urban design, and the ever-changing planning system.

John Stooke is a Swindonian through and through. In 1871 his great-grandfather migrated to Swindon from Devon for secure and better paid industrial work. John has been a Business Manager, Consultant and remains MD of his own company. He was a Borough Councillor, chaired his Local Council, Community Associations and has been active in local politics for more than 50 years. He regularly lectures on Swindon's history and is involved in the committees of many local societies. Having lost two children to poor mental health, in 2022 he set up and presently Chairs a successful community mental health support charity, 'The Kelly Foundation'.

ACKNOWLEDGEMENTS

Proof reader: Freda Garrahan
Katie Ackrill, Museum and Art Swindon.
Jenny Ackrill, Darryl Moody and Sara Steel, Local Studies Unit, Swindon Central Library.
Peter Benson, Photographer and former Arts Lecturer, Swindon College.
Iain Borden, Bartlett School of Architecture, University College London.
Janet Byrne, Local Studies Supervisor, Rochdale Boroughwide Cultural Trust.
Hertford College, Oxford University.
Neil Parkinson, Archives & Collections Manager, Royal College of Art, London.
Lucy Neville, the Royal College of Arts.
The Swindon Heritage Preservation Trust.
The Wiltshire and Swindon History Centre at Chippenham.

I

Introduction

by Philip Garrahan

'There was once a village on a hill called Swindon. It was in a farming area with no major towns nearby. Then in 1841 the railway came and changed everything. This almost didn't happen, as the original plan took the railway further south. When this changed, Swindon's future was sealed. It soon became much more than a small station. The Great Western Railway chose Swindon for making locomotives and carriages, guaranteeing rapid growth and employment.

This began a century of success in the age of steam. As the country modernised, Swindon developed a global reputation for engineering excellence. During the 1930s, its railway factory made three locomotives a week. The town and the railway served each other. As the town grew, few things happened that were not related to the Great Western Railway.'
(From the exhibition Art on Our Doorstep: Unlocking Scenes of Wellbeing, Industry and Creativity. Museum and Art Swindon, 2025.)

Background

THE EMERGENCE AND dominance of steam railways has been well documented by historians interested in the pivotal role played by transport in the industrial revolution. This role was heightened by the success of companies such as the Great Western Railway (GWR). The company was given permission by Parliament in 1835 to build its major line to the west. Swindon Junction, in the countryside and near the old settlement of the same name, was opened in 1841 on the London to Bristol line. To begin with, this location served two purposes: it allowed passengers to take refreshments midway in their four hour journey; and, it met the need to substitute the lighter engines using the relatively flat line from London with heavier ones that could cope with the increased gradients further to the south and west. However, the importance of the Junction rose in accordance with the public demand for rail travel, which in turn demanded more steam engines. Rather than continuing to purchase these from elsewhere in the country, a decision was quickly made to manufacture them in Swindon. The first steam trains were soon produced there and this marked the beginning of heavy engineering and manufacturing in Swindon. The population expanded to match the growing demand for labour in the local economy. The New and Old towns merged as the population increased from a few thousand in 1840 to 40,000+ by the turn of the century.

This book is about the social history of this industrial boom town in a rural county in England. However, it is less about the trains themselves and more about the lives of those who had jobs in their production. A premise of the book is that the industrial revolution brought social as much as mechanical engineering to people's lives. The GWR made Swindon in Wiltshire its own in the manner of other company towns and Swindon principally became known for its locomotive engineering factory. Of course, the transformational changes of rapid urbanisation and the making of an industrial workforce were widespread phenomena in the country. But Swindon is exceptional in the subsequent integration of these broader economic and industrial forces into complete social and cultural systems. These outlasted most others in comparable places and have had more profound consequences for national policies. They are the subject of this book, which broadly covers the age of steam from the mid-nineteenth to the mid-twentieth centuries.

The GWR locomotive engineering factory (the Works) opened in 1843 with 140 employees and this number grew in a decade to over 2,000. Because it was a greenfield development with no heavy industry in the locality, many skilled people were recruited from all over the country to join the Works. By the 1930s the whole Works site covered over 300 acres and had the extraordinary capacity to manufacture three locomotives a week together with goods and passenger carriages. A century after the railway line came to Swindon, the town had a global reputation for its manufacturing excellence and skills. However, there is a deficit in the literature about the social engineering that matched this. The social institutions and practices that developed in Swindon are, '… not the means of production, but part of the infrastructure that makes production possible' (Porteous)

The authors of this book have drawn upon original research to help fill the gap in our understanding of social change in Swindon with vivid accounts of Swindon's industrial and social life in the age of steam. Although the empirical evidence is about a single place in the railway industry, a key feature is the experience of Swindon and its people as it expanded rapidly. Swindon was transformed from a small township in rural Wiltshire into a full-blown company town by the turn of the twentieth century. For this to happen it was necessary to house and provision its entirely new workforce and to improve its public health at a time when ineffective water and sewage provision typically led to outbreaks of deadly diseases.

The chapters that follow explain how this experience both conformed to a broader national pattern of company towns and at the same time defined Swindon's case as compellingly exceptional. The GWR's dominance over employment was mirrored in its influence over every aspect of life and culture in the town. This is best understood as an adaptive and evolving combination of factors in which Swindon and the GWR might seem interchangeable to the outside observer. Their relationship was born of shared experiences over several generations. As the outbreak of war approached in 1939, some 14,000 of Swindon's 40,000 strong population entered the Works every day. This meant that in the first half of the twentieth century almost every worker in Swindon was directly, and to an extent indirectly, employed by the GWR.

Where rapid urban growth of this kind was transplanted to rural settings such as Wiltshire, ideas of space and power intersected. Newly created rural industrial towns like Swindon were proletarian communities geographically separated from major urban centres and so were peripheral to mainstream bourgeois thinking. They were constructed around an economic monoculture characterised by reliance on a single industry, basic educational provision and limited social mobility. In these respects the closest nineteenth century parallel to Swindon is probably the rural colliery town. Their schools functioned to prepare boys for manual employment and girls mostly for domestic work. Such rural industrial settlements were close-knit occupational places, with strong group norms in the face of demanding manual labour and single-minded employers. Because they existed in such spatially defined settings, some have characterised them as inward-looking in social and cultural terms. This book takes a different view by emphasising the substantial social cohesion and progressive qualities that resulted from shared community values and collective cooperation in Swindon. These in turn led to many community opportunities for cultural and social engagement including traditional music hall entertainment, dancing, gardening and sporting clubs, as well as fine art and opera.

In Swindon, there were different forms of collectivism and mutual aid that inspired and sustained worker initiatives over many decades. Examples include the Mechanic's Institute, the Library, the Swimming Baths, the Medical Fund Society and so on. Together these were the scaffold on which the town's modern education, health, leisure and welfare services were built. There are complex interrelationships at play here and a single book could not claim to be exhaustive about the social complexities involved. While there is much investigation and research still to be done on this subject, there are several broad contextual themes underpinning the book to note at the outset.

Firstly, there is the planning context and the physical construction of the London to Bristol railway. This was led by Isambard Kingdom Brunel, who personally surveyed the route and made several changes in the face of objections raised in Parliament by landowners. The preferred option took the line south of Marlborough, but when an alternative was needed the choice of Swindon was made. Without this, the history of Swindon would have followed an entirely different path. Both options had nearby canals to provide water and the transport of coal, as well as key railway junctions. The expansion of the railway highlights government's laissez-faire stance about the rapid industrialisation and urbanisation of society, in which the modern forms of transport played not an ancillary but a central role. In the mid-nineteenth century, there was no conception of the State as the comprehensive planning and regulatory authority that we know today. Historians have written extensively about how this changed, with the railway sector continuing to play its part in the country's development. The railways were brought into public ownership in 1948 as state involvement in the economy grew and were privatised five decades later when neo-liberal ideologies prevailed.

Another key contextual theme is of more interest to local historians who have studied the rise of population centres resulting from industrialisation. Other new industries in rural areas had to provide accommodation from scratch to house migrating workers, as in Swindon. Family-owned businesses were often at the heart of the growth in company towns. Parallels may be drawn across the wider economic spectrum with the Cadbury, Saltaire and other developments of this kind. In the specific case of the railway industry, company housing has been studied in Crewe, York and elsewhere. However, there is surprisingly little in this literature about Swindon, a fault which this book aims to remedy.

Finally, there is the political element of these relationships to be accounted for. Company towns have often been said to exemplify paternalistic and benevolent employers, who could at the same time be motivated to exploit employees for the maximum return on their investment. When accommodation and social support were provided by the employer, workers could experience hitherto unsurpassed standards of housing and education - as well as the benefits of reliably regular employment. Some workers in counties like Wiltshire previously had been dependent on the vagaries of low paid, seasonal agricultural jobs. In this era, the novelty of factory life seemed to raise the bar with the prospect of all year round, permanent and better paid employment. Of course, the darker side of this set up was that a workforce of healthier individuals whose housing was tied to the job was disproportionately of benefit to the employer. Nothing came for free in the industrial market economy and no more so then, than today.

These themes which match social with mechanical engineering and their political implications demand much more attention than is feasible in a short collection like the one in this book. It is more than just fine detail that local democratic practices operated in towns like Swindon significantly before the extensions to a universal franchise in national parliamentary elections happened. Therefore, the longer term aim of this book is to generate more scholarly research into Swindon's industrial past and this is especially important now that the town's heritage sector is giving so much emphasis to nostalgic references to the age of steam. In the meantime, the 'Delving Deeper' appendix following the book's substantive chapters provides a short annotated bibliography on some of these broader themes.

The Chapters

THE FIRST PART of this book examines key elements in the making of the new industrial working class in Swindon. Its first three chapters on the Railway Village, the Medical Fund Society and the Mechanics' Institute present evidence to assess their historical significance. Taken together, they portray Swindon as a distinctive example of the company town phenomenon - both for the progressive contribution of these institutions and agencies, and for their innovation and longevity. Having set the scene, the second part of the book has chapters about working life in a railway factory as described by a local writer and poet, the Swindon School of Art and its inspirational head, Harold Dearden, and finally about two members of the Swindon group of artists. These chapters together throw light on the experience of a new industrial community through adult education and subsequent art and creative writing.

It is fitting that the first chapter to follow focuses on the built environment, since social engineering began with the construction of the railway village in Swindon. Harry Lewis explains the beginnings of this fascinating urban space, which itself narrowly escaped demolition in the 1960s following a campaign by poet laureate (and Swindon ally) John Betjeman. The architectural properties of the railway village are a material reminder of the ambitions of the GWR's lead engineer, Isambard Kingdom Brunel. The grand designs conceal some awkward realities about poor living conditions which throw light on the difficulties and hardship of working life the early days of New Swindon. By focusing on the architectural properties of its village, conclusions can be drawn about the GWR's own corporate ideology and how its influence was brought to bear on the way the village was designed and built.

One of the earliest progressive achievements was the Medical Fund Society, which some would say was the most enduring and influential of the social innovations in Swindon. While it was endorsed by the GWR's management, it was designed and managed by workers who put a highly egalitarian philosophy into practice. Adam Busby's chapter tracks the historical development of this organisation which was administered for some time from the Mechanics' Institute (MI). Its membership and range of health and medical services went far beyond most others in the country and abroad. Its integrated provision of an extensive range of services is said to have provided the post-1945 Labour government with a blueprint for its radical welfare state policies.

Swindon's Mechanic's Institute (MI) was at the heart of the town's educational and cultural life for decades and because of this contribution it has a pivotal place in Swindon's social history. John Stooke's chapter catalogues the building in which it was housed and the often remarkable developments that happened there. Regrettably, it has been allowed to fall into disrepair since the 1980s, despite many campaigns to restore it. The building has become a metaphor for the equally significant neglect of the key social dimensions which it embodied. There are few resources to tackle the MI's derelict state at the time of writing, but this chapter celebrates and reviews the achievements and practices of those who worked in and through it to enlighten and improve life in the town.

While there are other first hand written accounts of factory working in late Victorian and Edwardian England, Swindon possesses an extraordinary and controversial example. This is by Alfred Williams, a local autodidact and polymath who for several decades was employed to operate a steam hammer in the GWR Works while otherwise teaching himself Latin and Greek and writing poetry. After early retirement due to ill health he became a successful chronicler of rural life, publishing several books about local villages and six collections of poems. He also collected the lyrics of local folk songs which otherwise would have been lost. His very personal account of 'Life in a Railway

Factory' is challenging because it leaves little to the imagination about the exploitative management practices that were indifferent to workers' suffering. Graham Carter's chapter draws on Williams' autobiographical record to bring the experiences of GWR workers to life.

The fifth chapter focuses on the artist and head of the Swindon Art School, Harold Dearden. His grandson, Philip explores educational developments in Swindon which benefited significantly from the foundations laid by the MI. The subsequent national art education curriculum responded to industry demands for improving skills in manufacturing design. Under Dearden's leadership the new Art School prospered, while also promoting skills in the fine arts. Two of the GWR workers taught by him who went on to professional careers in art are discussed in the final chapter of the book.

Leslie Cole (1910-1976) and Hubert Cook (1901-1966) initially took evening and weekend classes in art while spending their days in the GWR Works. Some of these classes were taught by peripatetic lecturers from nearby universities, often arranged by the Workers' Educational Association. Both men progressed to professional careers in art, but not before leaving a legacy of drawings, prints and paintings of working and social life in Swindon. This is art as social documentary which also serves to confront the often nostalgic emotions generated by recollections of the age of steam.

A concluding chapter draws some consistent themes from the recent research underpinning the previous six substantive chapters. There have been several previous accounts of the GWR's success and how this influenced the lives of people in the town far beyond the factory walls. However, these typically have been part of broader assessments of the Company's commercial and engineering successes, rather than primarily focussing on the social dimensions which are at the heart of this book.

Conclusion

WHILE CONCENTRATING ON their specific chapter topics, contributors were encouraged to engage with themes of common interest - albeit to work through different arguments or conclusions as befitted their individual analysis. This results in several significant topics being raised in different parts of the book. A few examples are: urban planning which affected both housing provision and the construction of social networks around the MI; the role of adult education that equipped workers with the skills needed in an engineering factory and also channelled their creativity in the arts; and, the question of whether the GWR was benevolent or exploitative, or both, in its pursuit of a company town. The chapters to follow concentrate on specific subjects to analyse the social changes that accompanied and were driven by economic forces. Together they make the case for an exceptional social order that was made in Swindon.

Reference

Porteous, J. D. 1970. *The nature of the company town*. Royal Geographical Society, 51, 127

2

The Architectural Legacy of the Swindon Railway Village

by Harry Lewis

Introduction

First established in 1841, the Swindon Railway Village (SRV) was a residential and social hub for Swindon and its Great Western Railway (GWR) locomotive and carriage works. It was an iterative project that was extended and redesigned to serve the GWR's changing economic and social needs. At the height of its building in 1891, it comprised of: around 287 houses, a large mechanics' institute, a market with capacity for thirty-two shops and standings for thirty stalls, a cottage hospital, an expansive company park, an Anglican church, a Methodist chapel, swimming baths and a medical dispensary. Due to its visibility as Swindon's New Town, the SRV cemented the GWR's material and symbolic place at the heart of Swindon. It also reflected the company's ideology and its mix of functional architectures produced a lasting societal impact.

This chapter explores the SRV's buildings and the ideologies of the people who designed and used them. The chapter begins by briefly exploring the company's ideology in its formative decades, before moving on to look at some of the SRV's buildings in more detail. The focus is on the years between 1841 and 1891. On 30 July 1833, a meeting of leading Bristol businessmen decided to form a company that would establish 'railway communication' between Bristol and London. After two years of wrangling against opponents, the GWR's Chief Engineer Isambard Kingdom Brunel succeeded in getting parliamentary approval for a railway between Bristol and St. Pancras. The act of incorporation received royal assent on the 31 August 1835. In 1851 the GWR operated 272 miles of track. However, by 1891 its network had reached 2,405 miles of track, having grown to cover the entire south-west, parts of the west midlands, and much of south Wales. Being home to the company's Locomotive and Carriage Works, Swindon blossomed with the company. In

1831 Swindon's population was 1,742 but by 1891 it had ballooned to 33,001. The company was Swindon's revolutionary catalyst. Swindon and the GWR would continue to expand into the twenty-first century before the company's post-1945 nationalisation and subsequent dissolution.

In late 1840 Brunel and Daniel Gooch (the GWR's Superintendent of Locomotives) established the new works in Swindon. They chose a greenfield site 1.6 kilometres north of the pre-existing town. Constrained by engineering concerns they chose the site in a few months, but their choice redefined the town permanently. Just another Wiltshire market town grew into the county's primary settlement within fifty years, replete with technical industry unmatched within the west country. To put this into context, the events preceding the locomotive works' establishment must be reviewed. On 13 September 1840, Gooch wrote a letter to Brunel of unparalleled consequence to Swindon. He explained Swindon was the most suitable place for the junction of the GWR and Cheltenham lines. His argument was elementary because of Swindon's position between London and Bristol; its position on the Wiltshire and Berkshire canal and the Cheltenham railway; and its low position above sea-level. Gooch argued that it was the perfect place for locomotives to stop before the mechanically challenging climb towards Bath. The GWR mainline runs southwest through Swindon as it dissects a stretch of the Wiltshire and Berkshire canal. North of the line, Gooch proposed four engine-houses to serve the Cheltenham, Bristol, and London lines. Gooch's designs would go ahead and on 6 October 1840 the GWR board of directors agreed to establish the principal Locomotive Station and Repairing Shops at Swindon. It was in this context that the SRV developed to house and serve the company's men.

Although the SRV is truly extraordinary, it can be compared to other Victorian industrial communities which can be split into two groups. In the first group are Britain's other railway villages, notably Midland Railway's Derby railway 'terrace' and the London and North Western Railway's Crewe 'colony'. Although these communities share their purpose as housing for railway workers and their families, the SRV's size, cohesive layout and historic social services set it apart. For these reasons, it is better to compare it to the second group – nineteenth century planned industrial model villages which provided residents with public services. Examples include Bolton's Barrow Bridge, the Wirral's Bromborough Pool and Bradford's Saltaire. Significantly the SRV predates these better studied sites by at least ten years showing that further research is important to raise Swindon's status as an important part of Britain's national story.

The Swindon Railwaymen and their Ideology

THE SRV WAS an extraordinary industrial settlement that sought to house and support GWR railwaymen (and their families) throughout their everyday lives. It is important to understand the broad convictions of, and pivotal figures in, the first generation of Swindon's railwaymen. Doing so provides a greater understanding of the buildings explored below. Perkin provides a summary of a growing class of skilled, articulate, opinionated and educated working men that was blossoming during the second half of the nineteenth century:

> It was they who: ate meat, vegetables, fruit, and dairy produce, lived in the best and newest cottages and filled them with furniture and knick-knacks, bought books and newspapers, supported mechanics institutes and friendly societies, and paid the heavy subscriptions to the craft trade unions.

Perkin's overview goes some way to help us understand the early GWR railwaymen who may have had a hand in creating the impressive SRV. However, it is important to understand the specific economic, geographic, and railway-centric features of the Swindon railwaymen's experience and their resultant community focussed ideology. The GWR was founded in a context of unprecedented economic liberalisation. This period of economic freedom started in the late eighteenth century and continued until the end of the nineteenth century. The Georgian legislature began to sell monopoly rights to create 'good roads, canals, and navigable rivers' to private companies in what Adam Smith called 'the greatest of all improvements.' The resulting turnpike trusts and canal companies shrank the journey between London and Shrewsbury from four days in 1753 to around thirteen hours in 1835.

The railway industry, emerging in the 1830s and 1840s, benefitted from the same liberalisation and saw a sustained boom called the railway mania. Countless railway companies emerged in this period of inventiveness, competition, and expansion. The success of the Liverpool and Manchester Railway opened in 1830 initiated a period of intense railway construction in Britain between 1837 and 1866. J. M. W. Turner's painting 'Rain, Steam and Speed' captures railway mania's essence, namely the ceaseless dynamism driving forward an economy. Britain's railways grew quickly through to the century's end as annual passenger numbers soared from under 25 million people in 1842 to almost 800 million people in 1890. Critically, railways were also highly invested in. Railway stocks represented 18.5% of the London Stock Exchange in 1853, a figure which rose to 49% by 1893. The GWR seized upon this, seeing the value in becoming a monopoly train provider that would vie for railway supremacy. Following parliament's passing of GWR's act of incorporation in 1835, the company went public and was listed on the London Stock Exchange. In this sense, the GWR was a clear product of Britain's unprecedented belief in laissez-faire economics. Throughout the nineteenth century, the company's main priorities were profit and market-share growth. However, its allegiance to liberal economics led to financial difficulties as well as successes. Such difficulties can be seen during the aftermath of the European recession of 1848. Being at the whim of the market, the directors forced Daniel Gooch to cut Swindon's workforce from 1,800 to 618 within two years. (Cattell and Falconer, 64) It was now clear that the GWR was a major company in the modern sense that profit came first.

Despite this, the profit motive was a boon for the company, especially considering the financial benefits of holding monopoly status. Even though discipline was severe and the work demanding, the company's economic success created a novel class of privileged railway workers. Such workers earned between 50 to 100 percent more than the average unskilled labourer in the early Victorian era. With this affluence came a system of shared ideas and experiences held by Swindon's railway workers.

The ideals of late nineteenth century Swindon railway workers stretched beyond a desire to work hard for the company. Their complex ideology mixed worker radicalism, self-help, religiosity, conservatism, and localism. Most of the GWR workforce's freethinking did not develop from the study of socialist literature. Instead scientific innovation, which led them to develop exemplary social institutions and ingenious locomotives, characterised their radicalism. For example, Brunel was driven by the desire to realise the benefits of new technology and modernise society. This attitude characterised the conduct of many of the Swindon railwaymen, since if they were to evolve the potentialities of transport they would not allow their community to stagnate. However, their pioneering progressive societies needed leadership. As hardworking equals under the same employer, it was natural that their social services would become democratised. It is hard to overstate this situation's progressive nature. The SRV's health, education, and banking services were democratically operated decades before universal male suffrage was established in Britain. However, a company man's rights to these services came with the responsibility of keeping them running.

The idea of self-help and responsibility was popular throughout the country due to the success of books like Samuel Smiles' Self-help. However, this mantra ran deeper in the SRV than elsewhere. Smiles wrote a biography in 1857 that established George Stephenson (widely known as the father of the railways) as the epitome of self-help. The stoical Daniel Gooch, the GWR's first leader in Swindon, put his own achievements down to unswervingly following his duty. The ideology of self-help was epitomised in the SRV through the educative self-improvement at the Mechanics' Institute (the MI) and the essence of self-reliance practised by the GWR Medical Fund Society (MFS).

However it would be an oversimplification to pin all of SRV's moralism on these earthly figures, for religious factors were also at work. By the 1851 census, an estimated 40% of England and Wales' population attended church on Sundays. A contemporary Richard Jefferies wrote that in New Swindon, 'every denomination from the Plymouth Brethren to the Roman Catholics had their place of worship.' Christianity guided the village's development through St. Mark's Anglican Church and the Methodist Chapel. This religious connection is deepened when considering that about three quarters of nonconformists were made up of artisans like the railwaymen.

Despite the existence of dissenting faith in the SRV, conservative values still held sway in Swindon. Daniel Gooch became the second (Conservative) MP for Swindon's local constituency in 1865. Swindon was then in Cricklade, a two member constituency. However, following the news in 1880 that he had been beaten to first place by the Liberal candidate, the SRV's loyal men ignited a costly bi-partisan riot. Gooch remained an MP for twenty years and projected his staunch conservatism onto the subordinate railwaymen. Similarly, the towering figure of Brunel, who had appointed Gooch as Superintendent of Locomotives, was also an unwaveringly class-conscious conservative.

An obituary for Gooch in The Engineer in 1889 states, '...his career is another proof that genius is [...] independent of opportunity.' Like Gooch, many of Swindon's railwaymen migrated to Swindon from humble beginnings. When the Swindon works opened in 1843, most

The Company Barracks 2024 Photo by Harry Lewis

recruits came from Britain's industrial heartlands. Gooch himself grew up at ironworks in Northumberland and South Wales. Countless families had moved to a growing Swindon, abandoning their culture while simultaneously distancing Swindon from its surrounding Wiltshire. Large powerfully paints a scene from his childhood in the 1850s when he and his friends visited the Welsh families housed in the company barracks and were delighted by their alien language. Swindon's railwayman ideology, having grown from disparate origins, was concentrated down and solidified by the Swindon work's unshakable geographic permanence.

The GWR and its railway works were fixed in the geographies they were built to serve. This created a feedback loop. Like other places on the line, changes to Swindon would reflect on the GWR and changes to the GWR would reflect on Swindon. The GWR's leadership were acutely aware of this. The company had both a Bristol and a London board to represent each area's interests. The GWR's architectural vision touched the entire region. Brunel believed that the 'railway could be rooted in the landscape [...] to become the grandest landscaped drive in the world and travelling along it was to offer a picturesque tour through the west of England.' (Brindle) This tour included Swindon and some of the new town's notable architectural features are explored in the remainder of this chapter.

The Railway Cottages

AFTER ESTABLISHING THE Railway works in 1840, Brunel and Gooch set about creating workers' housing on the opposite side to the main railway line. In around fifteen years, sporadic building had transformed the area. Before construction, the area was described by Richard Jefferies as, 'the poorest in the neighbourhood, low-lying, shallow soil on top of an endless depth of stiff clay, worthless for arable purposes, of small value for pasture, covered with furze, rushes and rowen [sic].' (Grinsell, 569-70) Nevertheless, in just a few years, the company had created a new village with 287 houses. Its influence is hard to understate. The people of Old Swindon, located a mile away atop the Swindon hill, termed the SRV New Swindon. It was new in many ways, as its regimented streets, centralised facilities and migrant population would have been genuinely novel. The questions addressed below are: why did the GWR build housing in the SRV; how was it built and used; and how did this use build into the company's ideology?

By the 1840s, 'The Railway Age had moved at express speed all over Britain, and as [...] the Great Western Railway system spread, so more and more railway engineering work was required, and most of it found its way to Swindon'. (Silto, 41) Workers were brought in from Bristol, London, northern England, Wales and Scotland. However, due to the Swindon work's rural and undeveloped state, the company had to rapidly develop new housing within walking distance of the Works.

Around January 1841, the company purchased land from the local brewer John Sheppard (for £400 per acre) and began establishing the village. Despite the GWR's acute need for a workforce, it struggled with cash-flow issues, having spent nearly twice the £3,333,333 sanctioned by the Act of incorporation. The agreement with local contractors J D & C Rigby signed on 14 October 1841 shows the solution. Rigbys were to construct 300 cottages at an average cost of £116 per cottage for the GWR, in return for an annual rent equal to 6% of their construction cost. For the settlement, Brunel originally planned to establish four cottage blocks around a large, open and pedestrianised High Street. His sketch of 1840 shows four blocks with hatched areas on each block's end allocated as space for shops.

The first cottage block was built in 1842. This is the only cottage block built according to Brunel's designs. This block straddles Bristol and Bathampton Street and is constituted by two back-to-back rows of 22 two-storey cottages. Each floor would have formed one tenement, and they have

Cottages on Bristol Street 2021 Photo by Harry Lewis

reasonably generous front and back gardens. Each pair of cottages has a central porch that shelters two entrances set at a 45- degree angle. This means that the two cottages appear as one larger cottage. Each porch is surrounded by a projected wall that houses two square windows with minute quoins on both storeys. Between each first-floor window is a decorative œillet, and upon the gabled roofs are stacks of four diamond-shaped Elizabethan-style chimneys. The contractor added rear kitchen extensions, due to the original design's lack of cooking space.

There followed the building of five remaining cottage blocks. The next block on Bathampton and Exeter Street (built 1842-3) went without a covered porch, drop mouldings, projected wall surfaces and window quoins. Then a block on Exeter and Taunton Street (1843) was built to similar principles but slightly enlarged. Next, grand tenements and shops were built on the first two blocks' eastern ends (1845-6). After this, development took place on the village's eastern side, with London and Oxford Street (1845-46) significantly departing from the village's cottage design. This is the only block entirely composed of double cottages, which were twice the size of a regular cottage. The front door provided access to a ground floor tenement, while a garden staircase gave first-storey access. This flexible design accommodated up to four families in their own private spaces. Next, another rather ordinary cottage block on Oxford and Reading Street was constructed (1846-7). The final cottage block built on

Cottages on Exeter Street 2024 Photo by Harry Lewis

Reading and Faringdon Street (1846-7) returned to SRV's basic cottage design, ending the housing's construction as it began.

The SRV signalled the GWR's successful embrace of laissez-faire economics. In 1867 it was called an 'emporium of North Wiltshire,' a veritable 'Chicago of the western counties'. (Silto,1 & 65) The company's successes were evident to anyone who walked near the SRV.

The SRV's social stratification signalled its reliance on laissez-faire economics. Writing as a contemporary to the developing village, Karl Marx saw increasing divisions in companies' labour forces as a hallmark of modern capitalism. They typically deployed subdivisions in their labour forces as a means of driving down wages. For the lowest-paid workers, overcrowding was endemic. An 1847 document signed by Archibald Sturrock (Superintendent of the Works) shows this by calculating that on average 7.5 people lived in each cottage. Given that many of the cottages had only two rooms, the lowest-paid workers evidently struggled with a lack of space. On the other hand, the village's skilled workers had a vastly different experience. The 1851 census shows that single families occupied six of the eleven eight-roomed houses on London Street. (Cattelll and Falconer, 75) This housing stratification meant that lower-paid workers would continually be reminded of their place within the company hierarchy. With local governments playing a minimal role in this period, companies like the GWR were free to establish social hierarchies as they saw fit.

Significantly, the village's layout also perpetuated spatial hierarchies. Its 287 cottages are set within a strict 13-acre grid layout. Each row was oriented to run parallel with the railway line and a nearby tunnel entrance on the

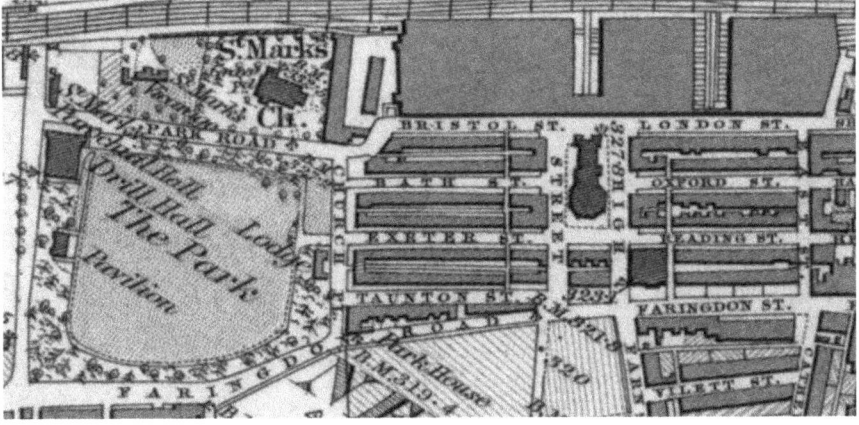

Map of Swindon Railway Village 1890. Wiltshire Sheet XV, National Library of Scotland Map Finder https://maps.nls.uk/.

village's northern extent took workers to the GWR works. Housing grids were commonplace in historic industrial settlements. Siting a settlement near a workplace and equipping it with direct access routes maximised the efficiency of the commuting worker and enabled workplace managers to surveil the housing.

> The grid is ubiquitous - used throughout Rome, sixteenth century Latin American colonies, North American settlements, nineteenth century cities of Europe, and the new town of Milton Keynes. [...] to form civil urban space, the grid is deformed to accommodate social structure, that is asymmetries of power. At key crossings large holes, such as the forum, are made. Variations of street width and of plot size are introduced, and axes are created. (Markus, 260)

Thus the key crossing was the High Street which acted as a forum in the SRV. Here, the Mechanic's Institution, the larger cottages, and the market reinforced the GWR's presence, ensuring the residents' good conduct.

Though the rental of cottages in the SRV usually followed market forces, the railway workers' radical beneficence still seeped through. Instead of wretched hovels which were common across Wiltshire, the GWR provided sturdy and hygienic housing. Significantly this happened around fifteen years before hygiene reform pattern books like James Hole's 1860 Homes for the working classes were published. Hole is often credited with persuading industrialists towards providing better housing. For example, after the 1848 financial crisis, Daniel Gooch intervened on behalf of the lowest paid workers and bolstered company rental revenue. On the 22nd of September 1849, Gooch, who ruled New Swindon like a Patriarch (Cattle and Falconer, 65), wrote to the GWR board and argued that the village's 23 empty and 17 partially occupied cottages were costing the company £11.20 per week. He successfully arranged a rental reduction of around one shilling per house or approximately half a day's pay. The size of the reductions varied according to the worker's income.

However, authoritarian conservatism tempered this benevolence. New Swindon was not peaceful and by the mid-1850s its population had swelled considerably. With this growth came problems that were intolerable to the GWR's leadership. The young migrant workforce had a reputation for rowdy, drunken behaviour and 'affrays and disturbances were not unusual in 1854. The houses in which they lived were so overcrowded, and the available leisure activities so limited, that the rough and ready conviviality of the beer houses and inns of New Swindon made a great appeal.' (Silto, 49-50)

The GWR leadership detested this reputation and involved themselves to control what they saw as misbehaving railwaymen. For example, when Daniel Gooch's brother William became works manager in 1857, he decreed a ban on snowballing in the village. He wrote, 'any person detected throwing snowballs into or about the entrance to the Works will be discharged.' (Grinsell, 39)

Brunel's initial cottage designs were laden with meaning. Their Jacobethan tropes should have been expected from Brunel who is said to have loved 'eclectically ornamental architecture' and 'remained a Regency buck until his dying day.' (Brindle, p. 8) While this partly explains the SRV's ornamental cottages, the regency obsession with landscape and architectural improvement also helps explain Brunel's design. Brunel can be connected with Blaise Castle Estate, one of England's leading gardens at the time. Brunel's appointment as the company engineer in 1833 was a pivotal moment in his career and it provided the twenty-seven-year-old with regular income for the first time. Until now, the person who selected Brunel for the GWR, John Harford, has not been mentioned in relation to Swindon. Yet, regarding the design of these cottages, he was critical. Harford inherited Blaise Castle Estate on his father's death in 1815 and Brunel was likely aware of the estate. This was not only because of his business relationship with Harford but because it was a tourist attraction. Jane Austen referenced the estate in Northanger Abbey in 1817 and when Brunel joined the GWR it was being reproduced in early postcards and was attracting high-status tourists.

Most importantly, Brunel seems to have learnt from the estate's Blaise Hamlet. The hamlet's nine cottages, designed by John Nash, had become a reference point for many people attempting to replicate worker accommodation on their estate. The striking mix of vernacular, medievalist and tudoresque features was widely repeated. The features consistent between SRV's cottages and the hamlet are as follows: ornate tudoresque chimney stacks, bay windows, lattice panes, generous gardens, and ornate porches. The hamlet allowed the Harford family to ascend from the middle classes to the aristocracy, which Brunel himself attempted to do in later life by purchasing Devon's Watcombe estate. By relocating some of the hamlet's eclectic tropes into the SRV, Brunel was showing his preference for the traditional conservative land-owning values that it represented. These aesthetically pleasing cottages faced the railway line, helping Brunel build the GWR mainline as the 'grandest landscaped drive.'

The GWR also honoured its west country links through the SRV's naming conventions. The street names on the SRV's west side (Bristol, Bathampton, Exeter, and Taunton) are analogous with GWR stations to Swindon's west. In contrast, the streets in the east (London, Oxford, Reading, and Faringdon) align with stations to Swindon's east. Overall, the SRV's ideological functions were clear:

> This unique settlement, built almost literally in the shadow of the GWR Works, was a self-contained unit. Its inhabitants could see and hear the express trains thundering along the main line, which was [...] a stone's throw from their cottages. They were completely identified with the Company, insomuch that they worked long hours in the Works and in return were provided with the necessities of life. The Company paid their wages, lit the streets, provided the water supply, educated their children, and gave them recreational facilities. (Silto, 39)

In conclusion, SRV's housing was established out of business necessity. However, their expedient beginnings did not mean they were built to low standards. Instead, the GWR took pride in building sizeable and attractive cottages through which its ideology broke through.

The GWR Medical Fund Society Hospital

IN 1892, THE Great Western Railway's Medical Fund Society (MFS) opened its architecturally notable Swimming Baths and Medical Dispensary. The MFS had been established as early as 1847 to mitigate the widespread injuries sustained in the dangerous railway works. In 1948 the NHS took over the MFS's responsibilities. Today, the building is called the 'Health Hydro' and is Britain's longest continuously open Turkish Baths. The building's civic and GWR pride can still be felt today because many of its period features remain despite several phases of change.

This section will investigate the healthcare provided by the Fund's Swimming Baths and Medical Dispensary through the following questions: why did the GWR support the swimming baths and dispensary's establishment; how was it built and moreover used; and, how did this use build into the company's ideology?

By 1876 the GWR had become Britain's largest train company and its rapid growth caused Swindon's swift operational upscaling. In November 1890, the Great Western Railway Magazine boasted that the Swindon works were 'the largest centre of the railway industry in England, and probably in the world.' The Swindon Work's employment figures show that 10,050 people worked there in 1892. By 1891 the MFS, established 44 years previously, was coming under strain due to the increase in injuries from the larger works. This situation was not restricted to Swindon. Medical 'problems were exacerbated in the mid-19th century as the spreading railway network and increasing mechanisation [...] produced a greater number of severe accident cases in rural areas.' (Richardson, 44) By rehabilitating injured workers, the Fund was of clear benefit to the company. The GWR supported most enlargements of the Fund, whose medical services were indispensable to the company.

> Very severe medical tests were imposed owing to the speeding up already demanded by mechanisation; those reporting sick were often discharged by the works doctors and little effort was made to find suitable work for older men or those who had suffered minor disablements. Work still started at 6 a.m., and sometimes continued for five hours without a break. (Grinsell)

The Fund was significant for another reason. It had for the first time in the village combined medical and hygiene services. Medical treatment rehabilitated ill workers, while the hygiene and fitness benefits which the baths supplied were crucial to the. SRV's ongoing public health. From its inception, the SRV suffered the effects of poor drainage and inadequate clean water. These problems were presented to Brunel by Gooch in his initial letter of 1840, which established Swindon as the correct place for the Works. The SRV's lack of hygiene caused endemic disease, including Victorian Britain's biggest killers— typhoid, smallpox, and tuberculosis. In 1852 alone, fourteen villagers died from these causes with an additional 400 cases reported.

Before the Fund's establishment, there were few options for healthcare in the SRV. The early Mechanics Institution supplied some facilities, and generous local doctors treated workers at lower prices. Nevertheless, there was no lasting solution. Gooch's letter to the directors in November 1847 pushed Archibald Sturrock (the Works' superintendent) to create a health society. The Fund was established the next month and started by providing lime and brushes to cleanse the railway cottages. By 1871, a cottage hospital was created in the village's old Crimean-era Armoury and provided 'one large ward with four beds, an operating room, a bathroom, a surgery, a mortuary and a nurse's house.' (Darwin, 28) However, the hospital's services quickly became lacking as the Swindon Works grew.

To address these issues, the Fund continuously had to expand its facilities, which included public baths. The pivotal position that baths held in the GWR's health and welfare provisions can be traced back to the company's beginnings. The first GWR secretary, Charles Russell, wrote a letter to Gooch on 17th November 1846, which referred to 'the present mania for baths and

The Cottage Hospital 2024 Photo by Harry Lewis

washhouses.' Proposed plans dated 29 September 1876 show that the fund felt pressured to enlarge its bathhouse on the SRV's south side. (WSHC) But this small bathhouse did not last long and the fund instead decided to establish a sizeable standalone Dispensary and Baths. On 24 February 1891, the Fund put forward a contract to construct new swimming baths and a dispensary on a large site south of Faringdon Road, facing the cottage hospital. The MFS chose architect John J Smith and master-builder George Wiltshire to oversee the work. It took eleven months to build and opened in January 1892. Over the next fifty years, the building was extended southward along Milton Road.

The building occupies the ends of Milton Road and Chester Street, which lay to the east and west. The main façade is on the building's north side and faces onto Faringdon Road. The building's southern extent is shrouded from view and has an access road. Moving through the Faringdon Road entrance, the Fund's secretary's office surrounded the original chamber. To the right of the entrance area, one could access the large swimming bath and three large dressing rooms. Ahead of the entrance area was a smaller swimming bath. From the southern end of the smaller baths was access to several urinals and a wash house. East of the entranceway, there are large rooms set around two big waiting halls to house medical services. For example, seven consulting rooms were planned, along with a large dispensary and a stew room.

The complex retains many of its original internal decorative features, including panelled doors, door furniture, architraves, glazed internal partitions and coloured glazing. (Historic England)

The exterior of the building is in a stripped down Queen Anne style. It is primarily dark red brick, while light limestone highlights its aedicula and keystones. Its façade is eleven bays wide and two storeys tall with a 5:3:3 bay rhythm. On the eastern wing, the five bays have an alternating pattern where the second and fourth bays are surrounded by two shallow pilasters which rise into windowless dormers. The central three bays project outward and have a central aedicule entranceway. The double-panelled doors rest on a six-stepped crepidoma, while simplified Ionic columns surround the doors. The columns' fluting occurs only briefly halfway up and the volute, rotated on a horizontal plane, extends upwards to create stylised fluted brackets. An engaged square column foils the central projection's symmetry as it rises into an oversized chimney. The frieze and pediment are unadorned besides a central cartouche, in the middle of the tympanum, inscribed with 'Swimming Baths/ Entrance'.

The Swimming Baths and Dispensary 2021 Photo by Harry Lewis

The services provided at Swindon's swimming baths and medical dispensary represent the SRV's most radical project and this is described in more detail by Adam Busby (see chapter 3). The remainder of this chapter will connect this trailblazing organisation and its real estate within the context of planned workers villages and wider effects on the nation.

The facilities the Fund supported in Swindon eclipsed those at comparable model villages. For example, Port Sunlight's cottage hospital built in 1905 had two wards, a small surgery and dispensary, with an equally small waiting-room for the reception of out-patients. While by 1904, the SRV had these amenities as well as two swimming baths; Turkish, Russian, and washing baths; dental surgeries and dental laboratory; and ophthalmology, chiropody, psychology and physiotherapy departments.

The baths and dispensary exerted a wider influence. Just over 100 years after the Fund was established under the GWR's supervision, it would provide the foundation of the National Health Service. Aneurin Bevan, the architect of the NHS, was greatly impressed by the SRV's range of available medical services and the progressive contribution system that supported them. He is reported as saying that these constituted a complete health service which should be expanded across the country. Before concluding, one must succinctly cover the baths spatial placement. The baths sit separate to the SRV's main grid system. However, by positioning it opposite the more entrenched cottage hospital, the GWR established it as an interconnected feature of the SRV. At the SRV's centre, the Swimming Baths and Dispensary's grandeur still succeeds in displaying the GWR's wealth and management of its employees health and wellbeing.

The Mechanics' Institute

IN 1843 THE MI was established by fifteen men with the object of 'disseminating useful knowledge and encouraging rational amusement.' Until 1853, the MI used GWR workshops as a reading room, library, performance area, and lecture theatre. However, it was becoming clear that as the Works grew, it would no longer be able to do so. On the 1 September 1853, Gooch delivered the solution to the GWR board. The New Swindon Improvement Company would be formed to construct the MI with an adjoining market-hall and the GWR would contribute in two ways. First, it would supply empty building land for the MI in the SRV's centre at a yearly peppercorn rent of 5s. Second, it would make a yearly contribution to the MI on the condition it provided technical lessons and a library. Before construction could begin, The New Swindon Improvement Company turned to SRV's inhabitants to raise the remaining £4,000 from the flotation of shares. If every railwayman enrolled at the MI had contributed equally, each share would have cost '£2 a head.' (Cockbill, 14) The sum of £2 was then equal to a week and a half of an average skilled worker's wages. Thus, Daniel Gooch's £50 contribution and other 'block' investments were vital to the organisation's success. The architect, Edward Roberts of London, was hired after the money had been raised and on 24 May 1854 the foundation stone of the building was laid.

In that year, GWR employees watched their grand MI built in the gothic perpendicular style rise in the middle of SRV. Once completed, it would become the SRV's educational and social hub for almost 150 years. The Swindon MI's leisure, educational and social programmes enriched the local citizenry as it became one of the most successful in the country. SRV residents initially had few options for entertainment, but by 1891 they had enviable opportunities. Through the MI, they could learn technical drawing skills, attend lectures, join the gardening club, and watch an opera. Additionally, the railwaymen democratically ran the MI for thirteen years before the second Representation of the People Act gave them the national vote. Within this period, therefore, the Mechanics' Institution came to redefine the SRV.

The MI Hall Late 1890s. RAIL 276/22, RAIL Collection, The National Archives, Kew, London, England

In the second half of the 19th century the growing opportunities for working class political and cultural expression, as well as for leisure, was not restricted to Swindonians. This trend pervaded the whole of late Victorian England.

The MI Library Late 1890s RAIL 276/22, RAIL Collection, The National Archives, Kew, London, England.

The second quarter of the nineteenth century, when the village games and amusements had not yet been superseded by professionally provided entertainment, left a gap which was largely filled by rational recreation and political activism. This tendency was reinforced by the influx into the new industrial towns of rootless immigrants from the countryside seeking substitutes for the culture they had lost and drawn to the strength to be found in co-operative self-help. Many of these people were illiterate and were attracted by the basic education provided by mutual improvement societies. (Radcliffe, p. 143)

The MI's construction was instrumental for adult education in Swindon. It quickly grew from a small lending library in the locomotive Works 'O' Shop to an organisation responsible for providing the Swindon railwaymen's technical education. It kept this role until 1888 when Wiltshire County Council took over the area's educational responsibilities. This would enable the GWR to keep cultivating talented engineers who would help it with profitable design innovations. An historian of the MI, Trevor Cockbill, argues that a significant minority of Britain's most adept steam locomotive designers had studied there while working at the GWR. This promotion of education for the company's economic benefit is consistent with theory. Educational institutions have been considered the most important agency for the reproduction of social classes. In this case, the MI would reproduce talented engineers and pass on their social capital to the GWR. Additionally, it has been argued that educational institutions are integral to social reproduction by instilling the right attitudes and behaviour. Thus, school leavers more readily comply with the disciplines of labouring when they enter the workforce.

The MI also benefited the GWR by encouraging rational amusement. Dozens of inns and beer-houses were opened around the SRV. With a population of only 4,876 drinking was a popular pastime for New Swindonians. A contemporary observed that 'publicans discovered that steel filings make [railway] men quite as thirsty as hay dust.' (Dunning, 110) This culture of public drunkenness was often met with company discipline like the punishment threatened in this 1859 notice from the Swindon Works manager.

> NOTICE
>
> It having come to my knowledge that many of the boys of New Swindon are very unruly and mischievous in their conduct, especially during the evening when property is frequently damaged and, (as on a recent occasion) life endangered, I hereby give notice that any person in the service of the Company reported to me as being disorderly, firing canon, or making an improper use of firearms in the Village will be discharged.

Before the building's construction, the MI desired to pull people away from public houses. On January 13 1845, Gooch wrote that the MI was a successful tool for 'introducing a taste for reading, and a distaste for the bad habits hitherto too often indulged in,' by 'young men [and] families.' Built nine years later, the MI provided a successful alternative to the SRV's beer houses.

The MI revives perpendicular gothic with solid and straightforward construction that looms over passers-by. Its most striking feature is the northern façade's dual turreted clock towers. Initially, an octagonal market stood on its south side. This appendage, and the main building, were roofed with shingles. As with many of the SRV's cottages, the builders used hardy Swindon stone for exterior walling from the nearby quarry. Dressings were made from Bath stone, while the interior featured Jurassic blue lias for stucco decorations. An article in The Builder provides further details: 'the roof of the hall will be open, the timber stained and varnished. All the woodwork [...] is to be simply stained and varnished (no paint excepting to ironwork) to be visible, and treated as ornaments.'

The Builder also explains the building's final plan:

> Part is under cover, with an octagonal roof 40 feet in diameter, with a public fountain in the centre. On the lower floor of the main building there is a spacious reading-room, with book-room and coffee-room, or retiring-room, attached. A council-room, dining-hall with hot plates, hot and cold baths, and housekeeper's apartments, are included. There is a spiral staircase in an attached tower leading to the hall, which occupies the entire upper floor, with a gallery and screen at one end: at the other end is a stage for theatrical representations. (The Builder, 346)

It is crucial to analyse how the MI was used and how it built into GWR ideology. As already established, the Mechanics' Institution promoted the economic interests of the GWR. In doing this, it reinforced the company's deep reliance and embrace of liberal economics. Another Builder article from 3 June 1854 confirmed the company's interest in the MI. At the MI's opening ceremony 'Mr. Simonds,' a company director, pronounced that the board 'especially studied in all things the convenience and advantage of the company' The advantages provided by the MI were that 'it was a unique organisation [...] as it made an exceptional contribution to the development of a mode of transport that has [...] proved invaluable to our civilization.' (Cockbill, 1)

Although it served the GWR's interests, the MI is still part of the radical tradition which spread throughout the country and abroad. Professor George Birkbeck laid the foundations of this movement. In 1799 he gave free lectures to Glasgow's working classes and by 1824 he had established Britain's first MI. Although Swindon's opened thirty years later, it still owed much to Birkbeck's original. MIs fundamentally changed the nature of British education. By relying on public subscription or wealthy benefactors to provide working people with a basic technical education and lessons on literacy and numeracy, they directly challenged the middle-class educational hegemony. The Swindon MI also shared many similar architectural features with the 12,000 others estimated to have been extant around 1900. Like in Swindon, most owned premises with a large hall for lectures and demonstrations, a library and reading room.

While the wider movement directly inspired the MI in Swindon, there are other influences. The SRV was far from the first industrial village to establish education in its centre. By centring education within its utopian cotton mill community at New Lanark, Robert Owen fulfilled 'his radical utopianism [of] work, education, social interaction, and leisure,' first promoted in his New View of Society (1813).

Nevertheless, the main difference between Owen's teaching facilities and the Swindon MI was the people who owned and ran them. It has been suggested that, 'power was the key for Owen [who] saw himself as exercising a rational, just, and benevolent omnipotence to choose both the means and the ends.' (Markus, 289) By contrast, MIs made decisions based on one member one vote as well as secret ballots. So, unlike the dictatorial nature of Owen's educational centres, the MIs instead operated democratically to 'respon[d] to various problems, such as lack of basic education, political impotence, and low social and financial status.' In this guise, the MIs 'were the harbingers as well as the agents of democracy.'(Radcliffe, 154) Overall, the radical engineering culture at the MI provided a democratic outlet for workers to fulfil their needs thirteen years before they would receive the right to vote in national elections. This democracy still had its limits. Although Minard Rea, the sensationally radical Superintendent of the Works at the time of the MI's building, tried wherever possible to sponsor women's participation, voting rights were restricted to New Swindon's male population.

Beyond its democratic role, the MI provided Swindon's railwaymen with an opportunity for self-improvement. One way to improve their character was to administer a successful society within the organisation. Thus, 'the Mechanics' Institutes encouraged [...] the large-scale involvement of ordinary people in a series of collective operations of self-help, [...] introducing many of them to methods of organisation which led to an avalanche of successful societies.' Starting societies at the MI became so widespread that within twenty years, there were 'horticultural societies, amateur dramatic groups, literary and reading societies, dancing classes; bands, choirs, orchestras; [and] sporting associations.' (Cockbill, 2-3)

The SRV's inhabitants also used the MI as a place to advance their social standing and financial position:

> As respectable as Divine Service at the established church, or the devotional exercises at dissenting chapels, the lectures and other entertainments at the local Mechanics' Institute became the place where the respectable and the socially aspiring [...] needed to be seen. (Cockbill, p. 4)

The most obvious way for workers to help themselves at the MI was to improve their lot. Robert Owen's 1812 business pamphlet shows how the connection between education and improvement became rooted in MIs. He writes that 'any characters, from savage to the sage or intelligent man, might be formed by applying the proper means.' The MI facilitated such advancement through its library, reading rooms, and public lectures. Alongside its collection of non-fiction books, the MI was proud of supplying a unique selection of serial publications. Its 33 annual report in 1877 shows that newspapers like the Times and the Daily Telegraph, and periodicals such as the Builder, Christian World, and the Popular Science Review were available amongst many others. Also, its lecture series went beyond providing essential technical education. The 18 annual report shows that in 1861 speakers gave addresses on subjects ranging from slavery's role in the American civil war to artificial memory.

Despite the educative radicalism of Birkbeck's movement, many contemporary commentators believed that MIs distracted working people from reformist movements. This might explain the otherwise conservative Daniel Gooch's presidency of the Swindon MI. Gooch clearly shows his distaste for workers demonstrations when recalling unpleasant recollections of the Merthyr Tydfil uprisings of 1831 in his diary. By supporting anything that would salve potential disagreements, he was lessening the possibility of a similar disruption.

The MI's spatial elements were also built into the company's ideology. As its leading force, Minard Rea always intended to use the SRV's central High Street. With its placement of the market and MI there, the GWR succeeded in establishing a commercial and social hub at the heart of its community. The MI's dominating power is architecturally visible when combining it with surrounding shops and the SRV's closed exterior façades. This was a common practice in the period. The mill owner Titus Salt is known as a reform supporter and philanthropist. His productive settlement, Saltaire, was like the SRV. While a long walk up a hill separated SRV from Old Swindon, the river Aire separated Saltaire from Bradford. Additionally, Salt strung out the settlement's mill dining room, shops, Sunday and day schools, Institute, almshouses and hospital along its central axis to assuage the lack of social facilities.

Beyond the local significance of Swindon's MI, there is the fact that it outlasted many comparable institutions. Opened in 1854, like Swindon's MI, Bromborough Pool's learning library and lecture hall had mainly closed by 1936. By comparison, Swindon's MI stayed open until 1986 long after others had closed. Additionally, the GWR was setting a precedent which would be adopted by others later. This was to contribute to reducing local alcohol use and rowdiness. In The Craftsman's 4 July 1912 edition, Barry Parker publicises Letchworth Garden City's Skittles Inn which served soft drinks and provided entertainment to promote temperance within the community Although

Parker's Quakerism likely underpinned the Skittles Inn, as opposed to GWR's productivity concerns, both the MI and the Inn aimed to 'formulate the higher standards of thought.' Overall, Swindon's democratic MI successfully worked in the interests of the Company's management and its workers and distinguished itself by its longevity

Conclusion

THIS CHAPTER HAS established the SRV as a rich and complex Victorian productive community that deserves renewed study. Its long-term economic success, its diversified power and its reliance on a specialised industry have created a unique historic area in Swindon. Despite this, it has been left underfunded and is largely unrecognised outside of Swindon.

Private companies like the GWR could create or destroy communities in the late-nineteenth century. In this period, the story of the SRV is hard to disentangle from both the wider town of Swindon and its parent organisation. With this acknowledgement in mind, the pervasive power of the GWR developed and sustained an ideology, which in turn pushed it to intervene in the lives of its workers through architectural forms.

Although this chapter was structured around the GWR's use of the village to assist its rational business goals, it was the residents who pioneered worker's democracy and cooperative public services while using the SRV's architectures as a tool. Company ideology pervaded the functional architectures that it produced. The SRV's cottages did not just house workers, they also denoted the village's hierarchies and expressed Brunel's personality; the MI did not just teach workers' technical skills, but it also performed as a place for a privileged workforce to express political views and spend leisure time; and finally, the Swimming Baths and Medical Dispensary healed and supported the workforce's bodies, but it also represented the village's collective pride in its radicalism and generosity.

To conclude, the SRV during the GWR's prime was a complex and multifunctional social and residential hub that supported the railway workforce and acted as a catalysing genesis for a regional market-town. The three architectural forms examined above have laid a road for its further study. In the light of the ideological foundations set out, this study could be extended to the SRV's other buildings, including its barracks, its public houses, and its trail blazing hospital which almost deserves independent study.

References

Brindle, Stephen 2005. *Brunel: The man who built the world*. London: Weidenfeld & Nicolson.

The Builder. "A Visit to Swindon New Town," *The Builder* 12, no. 591 (June 3, 1854) 289-290.

The Builder. "New Swindon Institution and Market," *The Builder* 12, no. 595 (July 1, 1854) 346.

Cattell, John, and Keith Falconer 1995. *Swindon: The Legacy of a Railway Town*. Swindon: English Heritage.

Cockbill, Trevor. "This is Our Heritage: An account of the central role played by the New Swindon Mechanics' Institution in the Cultural, Educational and Social Life of the town and district for over One Hundred Years." The New Mechanics' Institution Preservation Trust Limited.

Darwin, Bernard 1947. *A Century of Medical Service: The Story of the Great Western Railway Medical Fund Society 1847 to 1947* (Great Western Medical Fund Society), 28

Dunning, R.W. et al 1970. *A History of the County of Wiltshire*: Volume 9, ed. Elizabeth Crittall, British History Online https://www.british-history.ac.uk/vch/wilts/vol9

Grinsell, Leslie, H. B. Wells, H. S. Tallamy, John Betjeman and David Douglas 1950. *Studies in the History of Swindon*. Swindon: Swindon Borough Council.

Historic England. Health Hydro. https://historicengland.org.uk/listing/the-list/list-entry/13821

Jefferies, Richard 1875. The Story of Swindon. *Fraser's Magazine* 11, vol. 71.

Markus, Thomas 1933. *Buildings and Power: Freedom and Control in the Origin of Modern Building Types*. (Routledge).

Michie, Ranald 2001. *The London Stock Exchange: A History* (Oxford University Press)

Perkin, Harald 1969. *The Origins of Modern English Society, 1780-1880* (Routledge & Kegan Paul)

Christopher Radcliffe 1997. Mutual improvement societies and the forging of working-class political consciousness in nineteenth century England. *International Journal of Lifelong Education* 16, no. 2

Richardson, Harriet 1988 ed. *English Hospitals 1660-1948: A Survey of their Architecture and Design*. Swindon: Royal Commission on the Historical Monuments of England.

Silto, J. 1981. *A Swindon History, 1840-1901*, 20

Ville, Simon 2004. Transport. *The Cambridge Economic History of Modern Britain*, ed. Roderick Floud and Paul Johnson (Cambridge University Press)

WSHC. Wiltshire and Swindon History Centre. Turkish Bath House, Faringdon Street, G.W.R. Co, G24/760/410, Building Regulations Applications and Plans, 29 September 1876

3
The GWR Medical Fund Society 1847-1948 Healthcare from cradle to grave before the NHS
by Adam Busby

Introduction

BEFORE THE CREATION of the National Health Service (NHS), the people of Swindon enjoyed access to healthcare services from 'cradle to grave' because of the Great Western Railway (GWR) Medical Fund Society. The Fund was founded in 1847, 101 years before the creation of the NHS in 1948. Despite being ahead of its time, the Medical Fund is still not widely known outside of Swindon. One reason the Fund has been overlooked is that it does not fit into a simple narrative. The Fund successfully united different concepts and groups which could have easily been in tension: industrial workers and the management of the GWR Company; ideals of self-help, solidarity, mutual aid and paternalism; private endeavour and state provision. The aim of this chapter is to describe the Fund's functions, structure, development, and impact on Swindon. It will also evaluate its success, demise, and legacy.

History should start with evidence and not pre-conceived narratives. Fortunately, the Medical Fund has bequeathed posterity with a wealth of evidence. Primary documents, including its annual reports, rule books and written correspondence from the Fund's committee and sub-committees, can be found at the Swindon and Wiltshire History Centre (SWHC) and Swindon Central Library. These documents illustrate in meticulous detail the skill and efficiency by which the Fund was administered and flourished. The Fund's Victorian buildings include the GWR Hospital, now the Evelyn Community Centre, and the elegantly proportioned Milton Road Swimming Baths, a Grade II listed building now designated as the Swindon Health Hydro. These leave a substantial physical footprint in the town.

Swimming Baths on Milton Road now the Swindon Health Hydro, which has a Blue Plaque relating to the GWR Medical Fund Society. Courtesy of BBC Wiltshire Archive.

Furthermore, in 1947 the Fund commissioned its own official history by Bernard Darwin, incidentally the grandson of the famous British naturalist Charles Darwin. 'A Century of Medical Service' is a concise work which describes in reverent detail the history of the Fund and its development (Darwin). These sources are the principal evidence upon which this chapter is based. Keen readers are encouraged to consult these sources, particularly the primary sources at the SWHC, for themselves.

Origins of the GWR Medical Fund Society

WHEN THE SWINDON Railway Works opened, on 2nd January 1843, the residents of Old and New Swindon had to accept the wheel of misfortune and premature death as an inescapable reality of life. In the 1840s, dangerous working conditions, poor sanitation, an inadequate diet, virulent disease, and lack of access to essential medical care were commonplace. Life was often cut short and in 1841, the average life expectancy for men was 40.2 years and for women 42.2 years. The earliest years were the most dangerous. In the 1840s about 15% of infants died before their first birthday. For women, childbirth was also a significant risk to life. For those children who reached their tenth birthday the prospects were brighter: they could expect on average to reach the age of 57 (Office for National Statistics). Nevertheless, insecurity and the risk of poor health were facts of life. Apart from the workhouse, based on the 1834 Poor Law Amendment Act, which provided relief in conditions

GWR Medical Fund Society Hospital, now Emlyn Central Community Centre. Photo by Adam Busby.

which were such as to deter only the truly destitute from seeking aid, the State provided minimal assistance to the population. In case of sickness or accident, there was no welfare state to rely on; people had to pay to be treated by a doctor or depend upon charity. The residents of Swindon had to rely upon their own initiative and mutual aid to improve their health and quality of life.

The GWR Medical Fund Society was founded in 1847, four years after the Swindon Railway Works opened. Daniel Gooch, the then 31-year-old superintendent of the works, was instrumental in the Fund's inception. The confluence of industrial accidents; epidemics of smallpox, typhoid, and cholera; and an economic downturn had led to significant distress and hardship for the workers and their families. Hundreds of workers lost their jobs. Gooch penned a letter to the directors of the railway and requested permission to set up a fund to improve the overall health of the workforce, which would have the beneficent effect of inducing skilled workers to stay with the company. Gooch described the 'serious distress' of the workmen at Swindon and related the request of the men to the company directors to 'assist the men to pay the Doctor for attending all the families of the men, both in and out of work' (Peck: 55). Gooch's letter was persuasive, and the proposal was immediately agreed by the Board. The Fund was established the following month. Initially the Medical Fund provided for the services of a doctor who could be consulted, free of charge, by the workers and their families, at the GWR Mechanics Institute. Gooch continued his association with the society, becoming its President in 1857. Gooch's association with the Fund demonstrates the vital role which the GWR Company played in the Medical Fund. The GWR Company made membership of the Medical Fund compulsory for all workers; nevertheless, the Fund was organisationally distinct, and its management and administration were separate from the company.

The GWR Medical Fund was one of many 'bottom-up' organisations, known as friendly societies, which flourished across Victorian Britain, especially among male industrial workers. These voluntary associations sought to insure their members against the risk of sickness, accident, and death. Friendly societies were the largest secular voluntary membership movement in late Victorian Britain. In 1891 there were at least 4 million members of friendly societies as compared to 1.5 million members of trade unions and 1.15 million members of co-operative societies. By the end of the nineteenth century friendly society membership comprised between a quarter and a third of all adult males. Friendly societies can be distinguished by the nature of their membership – comprehensive (open to different occupations) or exclusive (organised around one particular occupation); by the ways in which contributions were redistributed: intra-personal (across a member's life-cycle) or inter-personal (between different members). A further distinction can be made by differentiating between whether the entitlement of members was based upon a formal contract or was solidaristic, based upon need. The GWR Medical Fund Society was a local friendly society with a restricted membership; its redistribution was inter-personal, and entitlements were contractual. Friendly Societies which focused on providing medical care were part of the patchwork of different and unequal services which characterised British healthcare before the advent of the NHS. The Medical Fund was restricted to membership at Swindon; it did not cover GWR employees located outside of Swindon.

The GWR Medical Fund evolved from the vast network of working-class self-help societies and mutual aid organisations in the 19th century. For example, there was a Medical Aid Society in Tredegar, hometown of Aneurin Bevan the Labour Minister for Health from 1945-50, who is widely considered to be the architect of the NHS. There was significant commonality between the GWR Medical Fund Society in Swindon and the Medical Aid Society in Tredegar. Both offered healthcare free at the point of use in return for contributions long before the NHS. However, it is important to note that the Tredegar Society was established 43 years after the Medical Fund in Swindon. Wider analysis of medical friendly societies has shown the Swindon and Tredegar examples to be unusual. Most medical friendly societies covered only the wage owner, not their wider family, and rarely covered pre-existing healthcare conditions. (Green) There were many other medical funds across Britain, including in South Wales. There has been vigorous and prolonged debate amongst academic historians as to the significance, role, and legacy of friendly societies. It would be a teleological fallacy to draw a straight line from poor law welfare developments and the friendly societies to the Beveridge Report and the creation of the NHS under Bevan. As the case study of the GWR Medical Fund demonstrates, the reality was more complex.

Achievements of the GWR Medical Fund Society

THE SUCCESS OF the GWR Medical Fund was founded on the self-help ethic of the workers and the paternalism of the GWR company. The Fund was aided by the large pool of workers employed at the Swindon Works. Employment at the Swindon Works rose from a few hundred in the early 1840s to 14,000 in the mid-1920s. The expansion of the factory made it one of the largest in the UK, significantly larger than for example the railway works at Crewe which employed about half as many workers. These large factories were unusual at the turn of the 20th century, only five per cent of the total labour force worked for firms employing three thousand workers or more. A large membership provided the Fund with a large risk pool and greater financial stability. There was homogeneity among the members of the Fund, as they all worked in the same factory, faced similar risks of sickness and accident, and lived in the same locality. This gave the Medical Fund a coherent purpose. The Fund arose in atypical circumstances, particularly in the south of England as Swindon had an unusually large number of industrial workers and had many features of a new town. The significant number of new workers who moved to Swindon had the opportunity to start afresh and support the development of new institutions, including the Medical Fund and Mechanics Institute, which would serve their needs.

The purpose of the GWR Medical Fund, as articulated in its Rule Book, was 'to provide for the Members and their families… medical and surgical attendance and medicine,' and to promote the 'health of its members and their families'. The benefits of membership entitled all members and their families to treatment from the medical staff of the Fund and the Dispensary. The Fund offered the following services:

> '(1) Accident Hospital. (2) Tickets of Admission to various Hospitals and to Convalescent Homes. (3) Washing and Turkish Baths. (4) Swimming Baths.

(5) Surgical, Sanitary and Dental Appliances. (6) Artificial Limbs and Surgical Appliances for cases of accident or deformity. (7) Invalid Chairs... (8) Lime, Lime Brushes and Disinfectants. (9) Lectures on Health.' (WSHC: 1908 Fund Rule Book)

The Fund's committee was also responsible for visiting 'once at least every month, the cottages belonging to the Great Western Railway Company, and occupied by Members of the Society' to ensure they were in good condition. These were an impressive array of services and benefits to be offered to industrial workers long before the NHS. The Fund covered not only accidents and emergencies but also specialist provision, preventive services, recreational facilities, and rehabilitative care. This was unusual in this period, since most medical friendly societies did not normally insure against the cost of surgical and other specialist interventions. The fact that the Fund provided comprehensive services demonstrates the workers had a holistic view of healthcare; and, that the Fund promoted and enabled a healthy, clean and active life. The co-ordination of services and efficiency of delivery demonstrates the achievements which working-class people could and did achieve. This was all achieved before the advent of the 20th century welfare state.

Solidarity between its members was at the core of the GWR Medical Fund Society. The Fund was based upon the principle of progressive contributory insurance. Table 1 below illustrates the rates of contribution for the different categories of members based on the Fund's 1879 Rule Book.

Type of Member	Contribution per week
Single receiving less than 10s per week	1 ½ d.
Single receiving between 10s and 18s per week	2 ½ d.
Single receiving 18s or upward per week	3 d.
Married less than 20s per week	3 ½ d.
Married 20s or upward per week	4 d.
Widows of deceased members	1 d.
Retired members	2 d.

Table 1: Rates of contribution for different members of the GWR Medical Fund.

The economically progressive different rates of contribution, particularly the discounted rates for retired members and widows of deceased members, illustrate that the Fund practiced the principles of solidarity and mutual aid.

These varying contribution rates were chosen by the membership through its democratic committee structure and not imposed by the GWR Company. The redistribution between the membership was made possible by the large and growing pool of members as the works expanded. This demonstrates the right conditions needed to be in place to enable the Fund to thrive and that in different circumstances it would not have had the resources or large enough risk pool to survive. It is striking, however, that the workers at Swindon Railway Works chose to operate as part of one Medical Fund, rather than opting for the creation of smaller Funds by job type or function, as was common in other industrial communities. The success of the Fund at building and retaining a large and diverse membership as the works expanded was crucial for its long-term expansion and development. As the railway works expanded new workers found it natural to join an existing and thriving organisation, rather than seeking to build smaller niche providers. The benefits of economies of scale, a larger risk pool, and solidarity between workers and the wider community are also contributory causal reasons for the Fund's development and success.

Organisation and Management of the Medical Fund Society

THE MEDICAL FUND was a democratic institution in which the membership elected the officials who ran the Society. The 1879 Rule Book stated that 'the committee of management, Treasurer, and Secretary, shall be elected by ballot, and remain in office for one year'. The fact the elections were annual is significant because it meant that there was a regular point of contact between the membership and management of the Fund. The management could be regularly held to account by the members and therefore had to pay attention to the views and interests of the membership. Annual elections meant it was difficult for the electors and elected to become disconnected. Over the course of a member's career, they had multiple opportunities to vote for their representatives on the committee meaning that democratic participation was at the heart of the workings of the Fund. Elections at the Fund were contested and had high turnouts.

The elections for the Fund worked through members voting for representatives for the department of the factory they worked in, like a constituency system. This meant there was a clear link between the Fund's electorate and their representatives. The democratic nature of the Fund is more impressive considering that many of its members would not have been able to vote in parliamentary elections in this period. The membership also had the power to remove medical staff if they were dissatisfied with their performance.

This occurred in 1859 when a doctor was forced to resign after the membership of the Fund held a vote of no confidence in him due to dissatisfaction with the medical services provided. The democratic nature of the Medical Fund was significant because it reveals the agency and influence ordinary manual workers had in electing the individuals who ran their healthcare services. It shows that the members were in control and that the doctors and healthcare professionals employed on their behalf were accountable to the patients.

The Medical Fund Society benefited from skilled and experienced leadership throughout its history. Prior to 1884 a different chairman was elected each year or half-year. From 1884 to 1916 Mr Morris was the chairman of the Management committee; he was replaced in 1917 by Mr Brunger who would retain the role until the Fund's dissolution in 1948. The role of President of the Fund Society was often held by a senior GWR Manager in the Swindon Works: Daniel Gooch from 1857-1864, Joseph Armstrong from 1864-77, William Dean 1877-1901, G. J. Churchward 1902-1916, C. B Collett 1922-30, W. A Stanier 1922-1930, John Auld 1932-1940 and F. W. Hawksworth 1941-48. Mr Rea was the first superintendent Medical Officer of the Medical Fund from its inception in 1847-53. He was replaced by Dr C. W. Hind, who served from 1853-59. Dr G. M. Swinhoe then occupied the office from 1859-1907 (an unparalleled length of service in the Fund's history) and made a significant contribution to the Society's development, treating thousands of patients over 48 years. He was then replaced by his son, Dr Geo. Rodway Swinhoe, who served from 1907-17, but left in acrimonious circumstances in a dispute concerning pay during the First World War. He was replaced in succession by Dr W. Boxer Mayne from 1918-21, Dr T. Percival Berry 1921-36, Dr John Lowe 1936-46, and Dr A. Gibson 1946-48. Other roles of vital significance included the Society Secretary and Treasurer; prior to 1917, the Secretary was a part-time officer, being released by the GWR company for these duties. Notable Secretaries include Mr W. Spruce who served from 1901-17 (guiding the Society through the turbulence of the early years of the First World War) and Mr S. E. Walters from 1917-40. Mr Z. Peskett undertook the important role of Treasurer from 1878-1913. The continuity of key individuals, both from the management committee and medical staff, provided deep institutional knowledge and expertise. These individuals, and countless others who contributed to the Fund's development, are due the credit for its success.

The Medical Fund directly employed its own medical staff. Its 1891 Annual Report shows that it employed a total of 14 medical staff, including seven doctors and physicians. The Fund set the terms and conditions of each role and secure the services it wanted for its members because of its power and size. It had a virtual monopoly on providing healthcare in Swindon as all the workers from the factory and their dependents were covered by it. The Medical Fund also provided its members with access to hospitals and convalescent homes for specialist treatment. The 1913 Annual Report shows that the Fund had subscribed to 20 different hospitals and convalescent homes including the Bath Eye Infirmary, Bristol Eye hospital, Deaf and Dumb Asylum, Guy's Hospital, Ophthalmic Royal Westminster, Orthopaedic Hospital, and University College Hospital. That year, 619 patients used these services. To provide additional security, the Fund made several investments, a 4.5 per cent stake in the Tenbury Railway and a 4 per cent stake in the Llynvi and Ogmore Railway which provided the Society with dividend income. This provided the Fund with regular income independent from the contributions of its members or from support from the GWR. (WSHC: Annual Reports of the Fund) The Fund was a capitalist institution, investing in private companies, and managing its finances against its risk pool. This illustrates the ambition and resourcefulness of the Fund's leadership and members.

The Medical Fund developed its own facilities and premises to cater to its member's needs and ambitions. In 1869, Washing, Turkish and Shower Baths were provided for the members in addition to the Swimming Baths already provided. As the works expanded, with the opening of the new carriage works in 1869, the Fund set up a cottage hospital in an existing building in 1871, offering an early accident and emergency service for workers. Gooch donated £1,000 to the Fund. The Fund matched his contribution, which was raised by a rise in members' weekly contributions, so the hospital had an endowment of £2,000. (Cattle and Falconer) In response to developments in public health and sanitation, a swimming pool was constructed in 1868 and a block of washing baths in 1869, which was extended to include Turkish baths in 1876. From 1887, it offered a dental clinic in the Mechanics Institute. This expansion of facilities and services corresponded to a growth in the Fund's membership as the works, and Swindon, expanded. The Fund benefited from the upswing of a growing town with new workers, many moving to Swindon from across the UK. This melting pot of industrial talent, in the context of the Railway Works at the cutting edge of engineering and technological advancement, created an atmosphere of ambition, energy and drive. It is not surprising that an expanding town at the forefront of such advances also had an ecosystem of vibrant civil society organisations and a well-developed and innovative system for healthcare provision. This illustrates how the various aspects of Swindon's life were interconnected. Often the same people contributed to the development of the Railway Works, the Mechanics Institute, the Medical Fund Society and the growth of Swindon as a community.

The Medical Fund Society touched the lives of almost everyone in Swindon. The Fund provided its services to the families of the workers, which included members' immediate family and nephews, nieces, or orphans of members. This was a similarity to the Tredegar Medical Service, which also provided access to healthcare for much of the town's population. The annual reports show that the local schools used the Swimming Baths to teach their pupils to swim; for example, in 1906 11,005 of the 38,641 people who attended the Baths were school children. (WSHC: Fund Annual Report, 1906) Therefore, the Fund should not be conceived of as an organisation solely focused upon the workers in the railway factory. The accident hospital was an important service, which saved many lives, but the Fund also provided maternity and specialist services, along with a dispensary. This reveals the outlook of the Fund, it existed to serve the whole community, rather than a section of it. This suggests a stronger communal outlook in Swindon, than many other communities across Britain in this time-period. The circumstances of a monopoly employer perceived common challenges and interests amongst the workers and a willingness to co-operate between the employer and employees created unusual conditions in which the Medical Fund Society was able to thrive.

Relations with the GWR

THE MEDICAL FUND Society's success was inextricably linked to its role in the wider community and its complex and multifaceted relationship with the GWR Company. By making membership of the Fund a condition of employment at the works, the GWR Company provided the Fund with a growing membership as the works expanded. The Fund benefited from the status due to its association with the senior management of the GWR Company who often held honorary positions such as President of the Fund. In a class and social status conscious society, these associations and endorsements were highly valued and contributed to the Fund's legitimacy within the community and its social position within the town. The Fund benefited from considerable loans from the GWR Company: when the Fund decided to build the new Swimming Baths and Dispensary in the early 1890s the Company gave it a loan of £4,500 to be repaid in instalments of £225 per year with 2% interest being charged on the outstanding balance. The Medical Fund then applied for further loans in the late 1890s to expand the Swimming and Washing Baths due to the growth of its membership. In 1897 the GWR approved a further loan of £3,000 to the Medical Fund so that the total amount of loans came to £7,500. (Steam Museum) These sums of money, while useful to the Fund, were small for the GWR, whose annual wage bill for the Swindon Works in 1900 was £600,000. (Peck) The GWR Company's financial assistance to the Medical Fund in the 19 century was crucial for the extension of medical provision within the town; however, it was a necessary but not sufficient condition. The workers, through their democratic structures and organisational practices, turned these loans into positive outcomes for the community.

The paternalism of the GWR also worked in their favour because its support of the Medical Fund placed the burden for dealing with the accidents and sickness caused by its factory onto the workers. The Fund did not challenge the working conditions in the factory and by accepting them legitimated the company's actions. By encouraging and supporting the self-help efforts of the members of the Fund the GWR absolved themselves of their other responsibilities towards their workforce. Local historian Angela Atkinson has argued that the existence of the Medical Fund freed the GWR 'of all responsibility for caring for their workforce.' (Atkinson) The company was happy to support the Medical Fund to improve the healthcare of their workers, but they were not prepared to help their workers by improving health and safety in the workplace.

The GWR factory was a dangerous place to work as demonstrated by the number of fatal accidents. According to the GWR Board report, on 30 October 1894 the blacksmith William Clarke, aged 75, having been employed by the company for 40 years and 7 months, was killed by an engine running him over at the works. Other fatal accidents occurred in the next few months at the works when Thomas Messenger was killed on the 14 December 1894 and when Andrew Miles was killed on the 16 March 1895. Alfred Williams wrote that 'sickness and accidents are of frequent occurrence in the shed. The first-named may be attributed to the foul air prevailing- the dense smoke and fumes from the oil forges and the thick sharp dust and ashes from the coke fires'. Williams also described the many different accidents that occurred at the works 'chiefly scalds and burns, broken and crushed limbs and injuries to the eyes.' (Williams) The GWR was unwilling to accept responsibility for many industrial accidents. On 6 December 1905 J. Patton, who was an employee at the GWR works, lost the top of one of his fingers in an accident at the works. The GWR Board Reports state that the company would not provide compensation to him because 'this would have created an undesirable precedent.' The company claimed Patton was responsible for the accident and admitted no responsibility. (WSHC, 1907) The GWR did not take a benevolent view of working conditions at the factory and wanted to ensure it took as little responsibility as possible. These dreadful working conditions should make us consider the human cost of industrialisation and the rapid economic growth which Britain experienced during this period. The Medical Fund Society had to respond to real and urgent problems, but it could only tackle the symptoms of the workers distress, rather than the underlying root causes.

Employers used paternalistic measures in part as an incentive for the employees to stay loyal to the company and not leave for a job at a competitor. In 1912 one hundred workers from the Swindon GWR works left the employment of the company to emigrate to Canada to work on the Canadian Pacific Railways for higher wages. The GWR Company had an incentive to encourage workers to stay in Swindon, and supporting the Medical Fund was one way they could achieve this. Other railway employers such as the London and Northwest Railway Company, which ran the Crewe railway works, also instituted paternalistic schemes such as providing housing to the workers, creating sick funds and pension schemes which re-enforced the hierarchy of the factory, and promoting self-help efforts among their workers. (Peck) By supporting the Medical Fund, the company placed the burden of treating accidents and sickness caused by the working conditions in its factory onto the Fund and its members.

There is evidence that the co-operation between the workers and employers created a more consensual environment in which disputes could be resolved and civil society organisations flourish. The lack of conflict between workers and employers at the Swindon works can be demonstrated by the fact that the 1911 national rail strike did not affect the Swindon works which remained open throughout the strike. In early 1913, hundreds of men lost their jobs at the Swindon factory, which led to criticism of the company from the Liberal MP for Swindon Mr Lambert. However, the trade unionists in Swindon sided with the GWR and passed a resolution stating that the circumstances were 'not such as to warrant going to the extreme measure of a strike' and they accepted the promise by the Superintendent of the works Mr Churchward 'to give further rises and to improve conditions' of the workers. (Silto) The workers sided with their employers, despite the job losses, because they trusted the assurances of the company and did not believe that going on strike would improve the situation. This could also point to the weakness of the workers' position in relation to their employers, given the fact that the GWR was a virtual monopoly employer. The workers may have channelled their efforts and energies into the Medical Fund Society, at the expense of Trade Union activity, because it offered a better prospect of improving their lives. The Medical Fund Society never sought to challenge the fundamental power dynamics within the community and hence the GWR Company never saw it is a threat.

Before the First World War, the reforming Liberal Government introduced a series of social reforms, including Old Age Pensions and National Insurance. This was a watershed in British history and marked the increasing active involvement in the state in the lives of the ordinary person. The National Insurance Act of 1911 implemented a system of health insurance for industrial workers in Great Britain based on contributions from employers, the State, and the workers themselves. Part I of the Act provided for the provision of medical benefits for workers, including gaining access to free treatment for tuberculosis, treatment by a panel doctor when sick, and maternity benefits. Though the National Insurance Fund was held centrally, and there was an obligation on certain workers to pay into it, access to the scheme was via 'Approved Societies' who collected contributions, paid out for treatment and provided day-to-day administration. The GWR Medical Fund applied to be an 'Approved Society' so that it could continue to serve its members and deliver healthcare services; in practice little of substance changed from the point of view of a member or patient in Swindon. It is notable that virtually no member left the Medical Fund after National Insurance came into operation in 1913; the Society already met their needs and ambitions. The Fund was adaptable to the changing political and legal context and was able to accommodate the changing role of the state. As the 1911 Fund Annual Report describes:

> The committee issued in November last a circular to all the Members pointing out the effect that the National Insurance Bill was likely to have on the work of the Society. As a result of representations made by the Committee and others to the Chancellor of the Exchequer, amendments were adopted which to a large extent meet the special circumstances at Swindon, and as finally passed it is hoped that the Act will not prejudicially affect the work of the Society. Some alteration of the rules will be necessary, and it is believed that compulsory membership of the Society will not be continued; but the Committee have confidence that the Society presents advantages which cannot be obtained by any other means, and they hope that the great bulk of those employed by the Great Western Railway Company at Swindon will continue their membership.'

Like most British institutions, the GWR Medical Fund Society was shaken by the deluge of the First World War. The Fund was placed in severe financial distress due to the adverse economic circumstances caused by the war. Many of the fund's members were called up to the Armed Forces and its subscriptions and financial resources dwindled. With the management committee and members arguing over a proposal to increase subscription rates, the closure of the Medical Fund altogether was a very real prospect. The Fund almost went bankrupt but was saved, in part by the efforts of George Brunger (who went on to serve as the chairman of the Fund for 29 years). Brunger was involved in trade union activities an official for the Amalgamated Engineering Union and was also one of the founders of the Labour Party in Swindon, and served the party on the Town Council from 1919 to 1932. A major cause of the Medical Fund's financial problems in the First World War were the huge salaries commanded by the three senior doctors they employed who were based at Park House in the Railway Village. A special committee recommended an increase in members' subscriptions to meet the financial deficit.

The GWR Company had an obvious interest in the preservation of the Fund, again highlighting the commonality of interest upon which the Fund's success and longevity was based. In the midst of the war, thoughts were turned to future ambition. In the Annual Report of 1917, the Fund looked forward optimistically to a time when medical provision could be extended to the whole population, "state Medical Service will undoubtedly be an ideal of the future, but our present Society, properly organised and worked, could be a model miniature State Organisation." This farsighted remark demonstrates that the Society had ambitions for medical services provided by the state and that there was no conflict to the structure or principles of the Fund. The Fund survived the upheaval of the First World War and went on to prosper in the inter-war years, developing its range of services provided to its members. In 1920 the Ministry of Health agreed to pay the Medical Fund Society the full capitation fee in respect of all its panel, and the terms of service of the medical officers were revised in consultation with the British Medical Association. In 1921 a consulting surgeon, who was allowed private practice, and a full-time dental surgeon were appointed, and the dental department was re-organised. The First World War had seen a significant growth in the activities and responsibilities of the state. This had long-term consequences for the underpinning assumptions of how society should be organised. Whereas before the First World War the predominant mindset had been how individual and civil society activity could affect local change, after the war there was a greater expectation that the state should provide solutions to common challenges.

One area of expansion in the state's responsibilities was the growth of local education authorities. However, in Swindon the GWR Medical Fund already provided some of the services and discharged many of the responsibilities that Educational Authorities had been designed for. The GWR Medical Fund's 1923 Report noted that:

> it is evident that the benefits provided by the Society for the children of the members, such as Spectacles, Dental Treatment, Medical and Surgical and other benefits, are a very great boon indeed and the members no doubt desire it in the way it is done but it is evident that the cost if not borne by the Society would have to partly undertaken by the Education Authority. In most towns there is no Medical Fund Society, and no doubt the cost of maintaining the School services is more costly than they are in Swindon, and if we, as members provide these services ourselves, it is a relief to the Education Authority, but it has been felt for some time that some financial arrangement ought to be made with the Society for doing the work which is really provided for by law.

This demonstrates that the Medical Fund's services were provided outside of Swindon by local education authorities. The Medical Fund already filled a gap which the state endeavoured to fill in other localities. The fact that the GWR Medical Fund was so successful points to the heterogeneity of social institutions and material conditions across Britain in this period. Rather than resorting to generalisations, it is necessary to pick out the peculiarities and differences in local circumstances to understand the development of social institutions and the conditions of the population.

The Medical Fund rebounded after the traumas of the First World War and expanded its provision and quality of services offered to its members. The Medical Fund was able to navigate the increasingly tense relationships between the railway workers and employers, particularly the General Strike in 1926. By 1927 the Fund directly employed fourteen medical and surgical staff, one matron, one chief dental surgeon, one assistant dental surgeon and eight staff in the dispensary. In 1927 the hospital extension was opened giving a total complement of 42 beds, an x-ray department was added and a blood donor service established. In 1937 the Swimming Baths were expanded and in 1942 came a chiropody department, a skin clinic and a psychological clinic opened by one of the assistant medical officers with a diploma in Psychological Medicine. Before the advent of the Second World War, the Medical Fund looked as if it was in its strongest position ever with more members than ever before offering a comprehensive set of medical services to its membership.

In less than a decade, however, the Fund would cease to exist. This was a consequence of the impact of the Second World War which led to far reaching changes in expectations of the role of the state and within British politics.

Influence on the National Health Service

Before the creation of the NHS, healthcare across Britain was a patchwork of provision, with many children, women and working-class men unable to access affordable and comprehensive healthcare. There were success stories however, including medical funds such as the GWR Fund in Swindon, others in South Wales and services provided by voluntary hospitals and some local councils, such as the London County Council. Efforts for state medical provision had developed since the founding of the State Medical Service Association in 1912, replaced by the Socialist Medical Association in 1930. The first British Minister of Health, Christopher Addison, commissioned Bertrand Dawson to produce a report on the options for future medical service; his interim report was published in 1920 but was not implemented. The Labour Party supported a State Medical Service from a resolution at its 1934 Party Conference. Before the Second World War, there was a broad consensus that health insurance should be extended to the dependents of wage-earners and that greater integration between voluntary and local authority hospitals would provide benefit. The GWR Medical Fund in Swindon had already achieved this; in effect, the rest of the country needed to 'catch-up' with Swindon. The key question was how to deliver comprehensive healthcare, a method of funding and provision and the roles of the public and private sectors. It is notable that the GWR Medical Fund Society was not widely seen as an example to emulate, pointing to perhaps the atypical circumstances in Swindon and the fact that Swindon was overlooked. If the Medical Fund Society had grown in a larger community or in London, it might have had more national influence and significance.

During the Second World War, a centralised state-run Emergency Hospital Service employed doctors and nurses to care for those injured, and arranged for their treatment in whichever hospital was available. The Churchill Coalition Government commissioned William Beveridge to report into the future of social insurance and allied services. Beveridge enlarged his focus from his terms of reference to produce recommendations which would set the basis of the post-war welfare state. His famous Report recommended that social insurance was part of a 'comprehensive policy of social progress' against the five giants of Want, Disease, Ignorance, Squalor and Idleness. In 1944, the Conservative Health Minister Henry Willink prepared a White Paper endorsing a National Health Service, based on the principles of funding out of general taxation, not national insurance. The services were to be provided free at the point of use and everyone was eligible for care, including temporary residents and foreign nationals. The proposal left open the possibility for local authorities to control voluntary hospitals.

The 1945 General Election resulted in a landslide Labour majority. The Labour Government, led by Prime Minister Clement Attlee, embarked on a range of reforms, of which the creation of the National Health Service was perhaps its most consequential act. The new Minister for Health Aneurin Bevan decided that a new national state-run hospital service was the most efficacious option for the delivery of healthcare to everyone in Britain. Bevan also believed that the National Health Service should be funded by taxation and not by contributory insurance as a matter of principle. Bevan also did not believe a national system of insurance contributions was practical, despite the evidence of its success at Swindon. Bevan believed that providing funding through general taxation would be more economically progressive than insurance, despite the example of the GWR Medical Fund which had demonstrated that a contributory insurance system could be combined with economic redistribution within the membership. The National Health Service Act received royal assent in 1946 and the NHS came into operation in 1948. Bevan proposed that state provided healthcare would take over the voluntary hospitals which were outside of state control, such as the GWR Medical Fund. This was opposed by the British Medical Association (BMA), mainly on the grounds that it reduced the doctors' levels of independence. The BMA led vigorous opposition to the creation of the NHS, which was only appeased due to concessions from Bevan on pay and terms and conditions for the doctors. A fair assessment would be that the NHS was created in spite of, rather than due to, the actions of organised medical professionals.

Voluntary and private medical providers, such as the GWR Medical Fund Society, sought to influence the creation of the NHS. The GWR Medical Fund held talks with the Ministry of Health in 1944 and 1945 to emphasise the 'unique position of the society'. In 1947, William Beveridge and Aneurin Bevan visited Swindon to meet representatives of the Fund and discuss the implementation of the NHS. The Fund's Annual Report highlighted the active deputations it made to Members of Parliament, during the passage of the NHS Bill, to highlight the special status of the GWR Medical Fund and request provisions to enable it to operate within the NHS, rather than be replaced by it. In 1948 Bevan met Mr Brunger the Chairman of the GWR Medical Fund

Society to discuss the details of the operation of the NHS. Despite the lobbying of the Medical Fund, no special provisions for it were made in the design of the NHS. Its medical premises were nationalised, with no compensation like all other voluntary hospitals. The medical staff were transferred to the new NHS and Mr Brunger was given a role on a local health board. The independent operation of the Medical Fund came to an end; healthcare in Swindon would no longer be different to the rest of the country. The end for the Medical Fund was tinged with sadness and satisfaction that the services it had provided would be provided on a universal basis across Britain. The Fund commissioned Bernard Darwin to produce a book 'A Century of Medical Service' for the Fund's centenary in 1947, in effect marking the end of the Fund.

Assessments of the Fund's influence on the creation of the NHS have been contested. A Swindon Heritage Blue Plaque on the side of the Milton Road Swimming Baths states that the Fund was 'The Blueprint for the NHS'. The popular belief that the Medical Fund played a significant role in the formation of the NHS is demonstrated in the views expressed by Swindonians on the anniversary of the creation of the NHS, particularly in articles from the Swindon Advertiser on notable anniversaries. This can be seen as part of the collective narrative and memory of the town which was formed after the Fund closed and the way in which it was commemorated by its former members. As the NHS came to hold a central place in British society, it would be natural for individuals to draw straight lines between past provision and the 'road to the NHS.' This is an example of teleological reasoning, an explanation of events in terms of the purpose they serve rather than the cause by which they arise. It sought to explain the Medical Fund as a forerunner to the NHS, rather than an organisation that had value and significance independently of the NHS. As G.K. Chesterton wisely observed: 'one of the most necessary and most neglected points about the story called history is the fact that the story is not finished'. Rather than simply comparing and contrasting the GWR Medical Fund to the NHS, there are a variety of other reference points, other friendly societies, other models of healthcare provision from outside of the UK (many of which, such as the German system, have many similarities to the Medical Fund in terms of its insurance system and local autonomy). Healthcare provision will no doubt continue to evolve and change in the future. An evaluation of the Medical Fund would benefit from a wider consideration of different healthcare systems, rather simply a comparison with the NHS.

Clearly the Fund was involved in the discussion and lobbying around the act which created the NHS, however, Aneurin Bevan had his own strong views on how healthcare should be delivered, partly informed by his experience in Tredegar and his socialist principles. The NHS had no role for friendly societies or the GWR Medical Fund, so it would be misleading to argue it was an exact model which the NHS replicated on a national level. The Fund was based upon the principle of contributory insurance, democratic local control, and oversight of the medical profession, rather than funding out of taxation and state provision. The NHS did not take the model of the GWR Medical Fund and replicate it on a national level. The story of the GWR Medical Fund is more interesting because it demonstrates an alternative, at a local level, to the structure and delivery methods of the NHS. It is clear that the GWR Medical Fund could have been integrated into the plans for the NHS under the 1944 White Paper. This demonstrates the significance and agency of the decisions made by Aneurin Bevan after 1945; he created an NHS on the basis of his socialist beliefs, based on confidence in the efficacy of centralisation and his interpretation of the principles of the Labour Party for the delivery of public policy.

The GWR Medical Fund played a significant role in the development of Swindon. It was a shining example of the agency, success and ingenuity of the workers, in cooperation with their employers, building comprehensive healthcare services. The Fund was deeply connected with the Mechanics Institute and the GWR company and demonstrates the integrated nature of civic and local society. The Medical Fund Society illustrates that voluntary action through a friendly society could provide significant social benefits. Swindon's conditions of a single large employer willing to provide financial assistance, and a strong network of civic organisations based on principles of solidarity and self-help, provided the foundations for the Fund's success. The extent of the Fund's success is striking; other medical funds existed, but Swindon's was, if not the most, one of the most, comprehensive and successful, particularly regarding the range of services provided and the extent of the local population which it covered. The success of the Fund was primarily due to the efforts and energies of the Fund's members; they provided the contributions, structure and drive for the Society's operations. Whether the Fund was an exact 'blueprint' for the NHS, as the blue plaque on the GWR Swimming Baths states, misses the fundamental point that the Fund should be judged on its own terms and for its own actions, rather than arguments as to its role in influencing the development of the NHS. Bertrand Darwin concluded his account of the Medical Fund with a quote from George Eliot's Middlemarch, and I think it aptly describes the contribution of the thousands of members of the Fund over 101 years: 'the growing good of the world is partly dependent on unhistoric acts; and that things are not so ill with you and me as they might have been, is half owing to the number who lived faithfully a hidden life and rest in unvisited tombs'. It is vital that for a thorough understanding of Swindon's history, and the development of social and healthcare provision across Britain, that the GWR Medical Fund is not forgotten or hidden; it has much to teach us.

References

Atkinson, Angela 2018. *Secret Swindon* (Amberley) p.37
Cattell, J. and K. Falconer 2000. *Swindon: The Legacy of a Railway Town* (Historic England) p.113
Darwin, Bernard 1974. *A Century of Medical Service: The Story of the Great Western Medical Fund Society 1847-1947* (The Great Western Medical Fund Society)
Drummond, Diane K. 1995. *Crewe: Railway Town, Company and People 1840-1914* (Routledge)
Green, David G. 1985. *Working-Class Patients and the Medical Establishment: Self-help in Britain from the mid-nineteenth century to 1948* (Maurice Temple Smith) p.102
Office for National Statistics 2015. How has life expectancy changed over time? https://www.ons.gov.uk/peoplepopulationandcommunity/birthsdeathsandmarriages/lifeexpectancies/articles/howhaslifeexpectancychangedovertime/2015-09-09
Peck, Alan S. 2007. *The Great Western at Swindon Works* (Heathfield Railway Publications) p.158.
Steam Museum, GWR Board Reports and Memoranda 1894-1898, and 1905-1907
Silto, William 1980. *Railway Town* (Silto) p.40
Williams, Alfred 2010. *Life in a Railway Factory* (Sutton)
WSHC, GWR Medical Fund Society Rule Books 1879, 1905 1908
WSHC, Fund Annual Reports 1891, 1905, 1906, 1911, 1913, 1917 and 1923.

4
THE SWINDON MECHANICS' INSTITUTE
by John Stooke

Introduction

Swindon's Mechanics' Institute (MI) was founded in 1843 and moved to purpose built accommodation in 1854. Foremost among its founders were workmen employed by the Great Western Railway, but their efforts were also supported by representatives of the company. Historical debate has centred on the balance between these two influences, but from the beginning the MI was inspired and developed by the workers. In reviewing their contributions to the MI, this chapter also serves as a tribute to Trevor Cockbill (1930-1999). Together with legions of local people he campaigned ceaselessly to save and repurpose the once magnificent MI building. Swindon's MI was one of the last of its kind to be constructed during the Victorian period, but one of the largest and longest lived of its 700 contemporaries. Although it is now a sad shadow of its halcyon years, it remains the centrepiece of the Great Western Railway (GWR) Village conservation area.

The Village is one of the finest preserved examples of Victorian industrial village design. The MI was created to serve the expanding social and educational needs of men (and their families) employed in the nearby GWR Works, as the train engineering factory was known. Its founding employees adopted a large room over the wheel-turning shop for use as a library and a theatre hosting soirées and other social activities. When this space was no longer available, they established the New Swindon Improvement Company in 1853 which eventually commissioned the construction of the new building. Using Swindon stone with Bath stone dressing and costing £3,600, the building's first function was to host a fundraiser in December 1854 for the sick and wounded of the Crimean War. The new MI was designed and operated as a multipurpose centre at the heart of its community. Known to local people simply as 'the Mechanics', to the south of the site was an octagonal covered market.

A print of the The Mechanics Institute 1854. The Builder 12 (595): 346–347

Trevor Cockbill

IN THE MID-1960s the local authority considered demolishing the whole of the GWR Village in order to facilitate a new road layout. Local opposition led by the Poet Laureate, John Betjeman, caused a rethink. A lesser known figure was a local labour historian, Trevor Cockbill, who went on to become a colossus in defending the town's architectural heritage. He was both furious and bereft at the way the town's few remaining buildings of architectural merit had been allowed routinely to fall prey to developers -only for them to be torn down and replaced by modern brutalism. Campaigning was in Trevor's blood, and in his 1986 publication, The Finest Thing Out, he told the story of the first 30 years of the MI, a tale brimming with love and respect in equal measure. He had planned to write a second volume but after a hotel development on the site was given planning permission in1991, he burnt all his previous work and endeavours. It was very likely Cockbill's work that motivated English Heritage to award a Grade II* Listing to the MI in 1998, a qualification reserved for buildings of 'more than special' architectural and historical interest at a national level.

As an early convert to the MI Preservation Trust, he was disgusted that Thamesdown Borough Council (which preceded Swindon Borough Council) had passed over the opportunity to acquire the building from British Rail for a nominal sum on its closure in 1986. This led directly to private sector ownership and several and varied planning applications and proposed uses, none of which had any serious logistical, architectural or financial integrity. The consequence has been decades of neglect. Encouraged by Martha Parry, Donald Brunwin and others, including support from MPs and other local dignitaries, Cockbill gave a lecture in Swindon in July 1996. Entitled 'This is Our Heritage', it was a powerful presentation about why this building was more - much more - than just stone and mortar. The MI Preservation Trust has promised to continue his work, with the aim of providing a renewed, vibrant and relevant building that plays a full role in the social and cultural life of Swindon, just as it did when conceived in the middle of the 19th century. In a modern and expanding town of more than 220,000 souls today, is it too much to expect that we can, via Swindon's finest heritage building, restore, repurpose and recognise the work undertaken by our Victorian predecessors? As recently as 1983, Swindon's Local Plan stated 'The MI will not be allowed to fall into disuse or disrepair.' Yet, at the time of writing, this is precisely what has been allowed to happen. Cockbill died in 1999 and his account of the MI as 'the finest thing out' proved it was much more than just a building. For him, it was the embodiment of a community's ideals, rather than the bricks and mortar that housed them.

Photo of Trevor Cockbill at the Mechanics' Institute. Courtesy of the Swindon Advertiser

The MI was conceived as a vehicle for the betterment of railway employees. The subsequent New Swindon Improvement Company provided working people with opportunities for study and self-help, succinctly summed up in its constitution as being 'for the benefit and enlightenment of those employed by the GWR'. At its nucleus were lectures and evening classes, supported by a small library, together with social events. Driven by 15 or so employees, a section of the Works' O Shop (wheel-turning) was set aside for dancing and theatricals. Over the following 11 years, the MI developed a wide programme of education and self-improvement, alongside social activities and extramural activities. With the agreement of the company, these were held in a variety of locations in the Works and, as things developed, the original paint shop was cleared and adapted for dancing and other amusements, while the O Shop was used for theatricals alone.

Design and Use of the MI Building

In May 1854 Lord Methuen, Daniel Gooch and Minard Christian Rea llaid the foundation stone for the splendid new custom-designed building in front of an estimated 10,000 onlookers, a huge turnout even by today's standards. Gooch had argued for a 'statement building', reflecting the grandeur of his beloved GWR company, and was quite prepared to depart from Brunel's architectural concept design for the Railway Village in order to achieve this. Following the ceremony, around a thousand guests, with full Masonic regalia, processed to the cricket field in the GWR Park, where a great banquet had been prepared, and there they were joined by the Oddfellows and the Order of Foresters, each sporting their coloured sashes.

The building had been designed by London architect Edward Roberts in a Gothic Revival style and took two years to construct. The main block was of two stories, although externally giving the appearance of a single great hall, with buttressed sides of eight bays. The building had been specifically created to serve the educational, cultural and social needs of the workforce and its members, as envisaged by the founders 11 years previously. To achieve this it offered a wide range of facilities, including a ground floor reading room (with most periodicals and newspapers of the day), a small book room, a coffee room, a committee room, an operatives' dining room, and eight baths. Strangely, it did not include any classrooms, so the GWR premises must have continued to house evening and weekend adult education classes. The upper floor housed the lecture theatre.

Meanwhile, the MI committee was kept busy expanding the scope of its various activities. Pressure on accommodation was such that, as early as 1878, plans were made for a major internal rebuild of the existing premises and the erection of a new theatre on the southern extension, which required demolition of the adjacent octagonal market.

The market had been another important innovation, given the expansion of the workforce in what became known as New Swindon. This differentiated it from Old Swindon, a long-established market town situated nearby in higher ground. By 1847, two shops had opened in the Railway Village, but only a small

A poster advertising the 1860 pantomime to be held at the Mechanics Institute theatre. Courtesy of Steam museum

part of the ground floor of the buildings was dedicated to the shops, with the rest given over to kitchens, parlours and lodging areas. As a result, the provision of more and varied shops became a pressing need, and the market was opened on November 3, 1854 with 34 back to back shops and a further 30 tented market stalls around the perimeter. At its centre was a fountain which may seem like an aesthetic addition, but there were good reasons to have a fine water spray given off by vertical fountains in environments where cheese, meat and fish odours prevailed. The new shops also had the benefit of discouraging the raising of poultry and small animals in confined and insanitary rear gardens in the Village. By the middle of the 1880s, however, the market had become disreputable and under-utilised. Given that the original MI building was now bursting at the seams, it was agreed that a complete review of the situation was overdue.

The MI committee proposed that their sole future objective should be with educational matters and cultural and social activities that could be included under this general heading. These proposals were accepted by the GWR board, and legal steps were taken to liquidate the New Swindon Improvement Company. Transfer deeds were prepared, and arrangements made to repay the outstanding loan of £1,400 to the GWR. In December 1890 the affairs of the Company were wound up and a new trust established to manage the planned enlarged facility.

The trust committee lost no time in preparing for the physical extension on the site of the (now demolished) market. Architect Brightwen Binyon of Ipswich, who also designed Swindon's new Town Hall and several of Swindon's redbrick schools, was commissioned for this work. A large amount of construction material was purchased from the GWR Works. The extensions were opened by the deputy chairman of the GWR, Viscount Emlyn, on 18

The reference section of the Mechanics' Institute library, located on a floor beneath the theatre stage. Courtesy of Steam museum

March 18 1893. To commemorate this, the roads surrounding the MI building were renamed Emlyn Square, as it was felt it could be confused with the High Street in Old Swindon. The extensions created a much larger reading room and library on the ground floor, and converted the lecture hall into a conventional theatre. In addition there was a smoking room, billiards room, a bagatelle, chess and draughts room, a ladies' reading room and extra dressing rooms for the existing theatre and hall. Also included was a new lecture room, a room for the council and a secretary's office. Improvements to the original building also took place, with a gallery introduced to the hall and a new flight of stairs added to both towers, replacing the old spiral staircases. A new ground floor wing was built, flanking the west side of the building, while dining rooms and baths were removed elsewhere.

The GWR Medical Fund Society established in 1847 provided for the health and wellbeing of workers was not constitutionally part of the MI. However, it used committee rooms for regular meetings in the MI, which was an important administrative centre for both organisations. By the turn of the twentieth century, the MI was the hub of the social and cultural life of Swindon. It had a library containing upwards of 15,000 titles, a membership of more than 5,000 and was promoting lectures on a range of technical, scientific and arts subjects. It also hosted regular exhibitions of small models and appliances, including microscopes, electrical devices and 'glowing' lamps. It had its own band, staged regular plays and concerts and had negotiated with the directors of the GWR for members to be afforded special privileges for holiday excursion trains. These went to places such as Weymouth, Weston super-Mare and resorts in Devon and Cornwall. It also organised the annual Juvenile Fete, attended by 20,000 people in the GWR Park.

In its first 50 years, and largely through the determination of the workers, the MI had become the central agency in the educational, health and cultural life of what was a company town. When Trevor Cockbill praised it as, 'the finest thing out', he was emphasising the workers' collective and socially progressive endeavours. Alongside this, there was support from the company, in the form of the GWR's Chief Mechanical Engineer, Daniel Gooch, and Works Manager Minard Christian Rea, and from enlightened members of the community. The MI provided for real and practical needs and these were mostly suggested and managed by the workforce. Powerful men have taken the credit for the ideas conceived by others, and possibly Daniel Gooch was no different in this regard. He claimed to have begun the MI in response to complaints from the neighbouring gentry about drunkenness and disorder, stating: 'I got together those of the workmen whose moral character was superior to their fellows, and formed them into a workmen's Institute.' By contrast, Trevor Cockbill's argument was that the main driving force behind the formation was from the workers on the ground.

Trevor Cockbill gave his acclaimed 1996 lecture, 'This Is Our Heritage to the members and supporters of the New Mechanics' Institute Preservation Trust at the Coleview Community Centre in Swindon. He reviewed the MI's impact over 100 years on the town and began by saying:

> Some of my friends who are members of the Trust have been kind enough to offer me the privilege of this platform to expound my own belief, which is that the Institution, which began in 1843 with a collection of just a few books to form a small circulating library, became the most valuable and most precious part of the heritage to which we, living in this area, can lay claim today. It follows that any talk of the heritage of Swindon and its vicinity, any attempt to build on it, or to explain it, will be nonsense unless the Mechanics' Institution is afforded its central and proper role.

Cockbill emphasised 'vicinity' because he argued the MI belonged to the whole town and to its local environment. From its inception, the membership included people who lived on the hill in Swindon and in Stratton, Wanborough, Rodbourne Cheney, Wroughton, South Marston and many of the outlying parishes. He proposed that Swindon's MI was unique, even among other mechanics' institutions, and that, '... a roll of honour of the institution members, over a period of more than 100 years would contain, if such a roll could ever be compiled, a galaxy of illustrious names, the like of which no other local or voluntary organisation in the United Kingdom or elsewhere could ever hope to rival'. The components of his argument were that the MI's influence extended to broader societal changes as a forerunner of democratic practices; it was a leading influence in technical education and engineering excellence; it shaped the literary and cultural life of the town and impacted on housing and public health; and that without it the GWR railway factory may even have been at risk. These propositions together made the MI much more than the building that housed it.

The Role Played by the MI in a Societal Revolution

THE FIRST OF Trevor Cockbill's propositions was that when considering the early mechanics' institutions, which sprang up throughout the country in the 25 years prior to 1850, we are looking at the beginnings of something very new in British social life. It was, he argued, one of the most significant stories of our islands, one of the most important developments since the Norman Conquest, and of wider significance than such historical events as the Magna Carta. For Cockbill, these institutions encouraged for the first time the large scale involvement of ordinary people in the new industrial areas in a series of collective operations of self-help, introducing many of them to the practical methods of organisation. This led to an avalanche of successful societies, clubs, associations and institutions, which rapidly became a feature in all walks of life in Swindon and remain an important element in the town today. It is also probably true that a few, who may have been otherwise persuaded to join revolutionary activities, were diverted from such paths and were sufficiently amused by the writings of contemporary authors to forget their hunger or long hours of toil, or their wretched living conditions. People who might have been drawn to street demonstrations for political reform, were instead busy in the institutes, reflecting on the latest songs by Mr Mendelssohn or enduring lectures on the positive benefits to be obtained from the Turkish bath. This proposition deserves further research, but it is significant to acknowledge the mechanics institutes' achievements. They succeeded in encouraging a thirst for knowledge and self-improvement among the barely literate as well as the better educated.

The MI and the Development of the Democratic Process

IN 1825, WHEN the first mechanics' institutes were founded, Britain could lay no claim to popular democracy. In rural shires, power was principally in the hands of landed gentry who were also magistrates. When they joined together in quarter sessions, they assumed a role as a de facto local council. But things were changing. In 1832, a new act tried to straighten out the inequality between constituencies, but even then only about a half million people could vote out of a population of 14 million. Also, those voting had to declare their public allegiance to the establishment and those in authority could make life uncomfortable for anyone who stood against its interests. At the outset, MIs adopted the principle of one person, one vote and where necessary secret ballots on contentious matters. Also, most were administered by a council elected annually by rank-and-file membership. This is why Cockbill so admired them, stressing that these were the only bodies or associations at the time that incorporated such democratic principles in their constitution.

The institutes offered tuition in reading and writing not widely available to working class people, and they provided officers with experience of business administration and record-keeping. So, it is possible to make a direct link between the institutes and the growing acceptance of democratic principles and practices in the country during the nineteenth century. Furthermore, local councils, with their elections through popular franchise and working through specialist committees, can be shown to have followed the form of the mechanics' institutions. In Swindon, both the local Conservative and Liberal associations that eventually emerged owed much to the veteran organisers of the local MI.

The MI as Catalyst for Formal Technical Education

THE SWINDON MI retained control of its classes until the responsibility for technical education was vested in the new county councils by legislation passed in 1893. Before then the MI financed an extensive educational educational programme aided by modest fees, which most students paid. In 1871 it was affiliated to the Government's Department of Science and Arts, based in Kensington, and received some grant support as a result. With the assistance and encouragement of the GWR's Chief Mechanical Engineer, Joseph Armstrong, who had also succeeded Gooch as President of the MI in 1865, a valuable innovation was introduced: this was an early example of the now commonly accepted need to harmonise technical education with the progress young workers made through the workshops.

The MI also awarded scholarships for its own classes to those sons of members who showed promise at the town's board schools. Cockbill's research further told him that, in some cases, those who could not afford the modest fees were not deprived of opportunity and 'this was symptomatic of the overall kindliness and understanding that so characterised our Mechanics' Institute'. Prior to the 1893 Act, which required all local authorities to put in place their own technical education colleges, there were plans for the MI to have its own technical college. In a spirit of co-operation, however, the MI council handed over a complete package for the foundation of what was to become the Swindon College. This included the better part of a thousand part-time students; a wide variety of instruction courses and course work, each with its own proven and successful syllabus; a huge quantity of apparatus; and, importantly, a small army of part-time lecturers all trained by the MI and certified by examination by the Department of Science and Art. These educational and human resources constituted a well-established academic tradition, which was handed in its entirety by the MI to the town of Swindon. It was, in effect, a complete educational establishment in all but its own building, and on this form and scale it was unquestionably unique. The Swindon MI's pioneering nineteenth century educational provision was assisted from the early twentieth century by the Workers' Educational Association and university extension classes. These continued to be housed in the MI's premises and were accessed both by GWR employees and others in Swindon and its vicinity.

The MI and Swindon's Global Reputation for Engineering Excellence.

MANY FORMER MI members were involved in railway developments across a rapidly changing international industrial landscape. From 1871 until the handover of technical education to Swindon College at the turn of the century, Swindon's Works and the MI together produced a host of brilliant engineers. The dominant leadership of Daniel Gooch was firmly in place until his death in 1889, although this frustrated the flowering of accumulated genius to the extent that many brilliant men decided to pursue careers elsewhere. Under the stewardship of his successor, Major William Dean, a new but largely experimental series of highly efficient locomotives began to emerge. When George Jackson Churchward took over, a new generation of talent was released. The Swindon Works then innovated with engines such as the Saints and the Stars, which broke new ground and established the basic outline of British locomotive development until the end of steam traction. Rated among the leading international locomotive engineers of the nineteenth century were William Dean, Charles Collett, William Stanier and Nigel Gresley and Frederick Hawksworth. With the exception of Gresley, all of these were MI men, and owed as much to it and its methods as to the GWR. Gresley himself needed to call on Swindon Works engineers to understand modifications to the valve gear on his larger engines. Expanding this list there are two other graduates of Swindon Works and the MI who would be included, namely James Holden of the Great Eastern Railway, and John G Robinson of the Great Central Railway. Meanwhile, Robert Farlie, a pupil of Minard Christian Rea and an MI member, whose engines were the only ones capable of pulling mineral trains up the gradient from Mexico City to the port of Santa Cruz, also gained a special medal from the Tsar of Russia for his work on the Moscow to St Petersburg railway. Many more engineers with connections to the Swindon MI, including Archibald Sturrock and his pupil, Charles Sacre, also made their marks internationally.

The MI and Swindon's Literary Tradition

FURTHER EVIDENCE THAT both the MI philosophy and its building were stunning successes is recorded by Richard Jefferies, perhaps Swindon's best known nineteenth century author. He applauded the role of the MI in the town in his book, *The Hills and the Vale* writing, 'The great and well supplied reading room of the Mechanics' Institute is always full of readers; the library, now an extensive one, is constantly in use; where one book is read in agricultural districts, 50 are read in the vicinity of the factory.' The MI library predated by seven years the country's first free lending library opened in Salford 1850. When the new MI building opened in 1854, its library already boasted almost 3,000 volumes and an average of 1,500 books were borrowed by members each month. It also boasted a well stocked reference section. As Swindon's population grew, so did the MI's library and it became the centrepiece of academic learning and intellectual development in the town over the course of the next hundred years. It was not until 1943 that the local education authority needed to open the town's first publicly funded lending library as, until then, this role had been eminently filled by the MI.

This had a far reaching effect on the literary and educational development of the town. Some of those who emerged from this tradition in addition to Jefferies include William Morris who founded the *Swindon Advertiser* in 1854, was its editor for almost forty years and who published *Swindon 50 Years Ago* in 1885; Alfred Williams, also known as the 'Hammerman Poet', who wrote chronicles of rural life around Swindon and published his personal account of *Life in a Railway Factory* in 1915; Dr FH Spencer, who included an account of his boyhood in Swindon in his 1938 book, *An Inspector's Testament*; and Dr John Treherne, a Cambridge University entomologist, who wrote two novels describing his childhood in the interwar years near Swindon. Joe Silto, a lifelong servant of the GWR and later British Rail, wrote, *A Swindon History* and *The Railway Town*. These remain valuable heritage resources.

The MI's Influence on Housing and Public Health

IT WAS AS true in the late Victorian era as it is today that good public health begins with a sufficient supply of decent housing. The shortage of affordable, quality housing had bedevilled Swindon since the GWR began and was a major factor in the outbreaks of cholera and the widespread incidence of tuberculosis. In August 1868 the MI building was made available for the launch of the Swindon Permanent Building Society. This brought the dual benefits of more modern standards of construction and affordable loans to buyers. Most of the MI's officers were actively involved in the Society, which from the beginning followed the MI's reputation for trustworthiness and ethical dealing. The MI's auditor, William Hall, was appointed secretary of the Society and for many years an office in the MI was used by it for the conduct of its business. A number of the most influential and prestigious members of the MI at the time served on the Society's board of directors. It was responsible for many of the red-brick terraces that were quickly developed around Cheltenham Street and Gloucester Street and it also provided leadership for others, such as the Oxford Building Society, which developed the Queenstown area, especially Carfax, Merton and Oriel Streets.

Public health is not only about housing, however, and the MI played a significant role in the broader picture. During the economic depression of 1847, Minard Rea persuaded Daniel Gooch that it was a terrible time for the men and begged him to seek to remedy this. Gooch wrote to the directors of the GWR advocating for a doctor to attend to the mens' needs - not just accidents, but smallpox, typhus and cholera. The Directors agreed and a Medical Fund Society was formed by men employed at the Works in December 1847, with Archibald Sturrock as President. The men elected a committee and secretary, the committee deciding on the Chairman. Members of the committee relied on the experience gained in their roles in the MI. In addition to the local doctor, the Fund facilitated visits to hospitals in Bath and London. Later the Fund arranged for the Works to produce crutches, wheelchairs and rudimentary prosthetic limbs. Trevor Cockbill's research into the Fund's minute books identified a number of the men who had served on the MI Council and who quickly brought their experience to bear on the organisation and management of the Medical Fund.

These included Jonno Short and his successor William Richards. In addition, former MI council members Barefoot, Watson, Drummond and Dyer all drew on their experience there to lay the foundation for the Medical Fund's major contribution not just to GWR employees but to the whole town. In January 1865 and with the MI band in attendance, the schoolmaster Mr Braid, who was formerly first secretary of the MI, launched penny readings in the MI hall. The monies raised were set aside for the hospital project. In 1862, the committee had asked Mr Gooch and Dr Swinhoe to try to establish a hospital for the benefit of its members. Joseph Armstrong laid the proposal before the Directors in March 1871. As a result, the existing Armory and adjoining cottage were taken over with the Directors granting £130 for altering the buildings and then subscribing £20 a year. By the end of 1871, there was one large ward with four beds which was later extended. It opened in 1872 with an endowment of £1000 from the workers and a personal contribution of £1000 from Daniel Gooch. In this way the MI acted as the guiding foster parent for an organisation that became Swindon's most valuable export, arguably providing inspiration and a blueprint for the foundation of the National Health Service a century later.

The MI and Arts and Culture in Swindon

From the day the MI opened until it closed its doors in 1960, the building regularly hosted musical and theatrical entertainment, dinners and ceremonies, and dances and socials. Its Playhouse Theatre saw a wide range of entertainment and among those active in these events was Harry Stanley Fairclough, musical arranger and producer at the MI. For two decades he turned a Wiltshire town into a leading centre of opera, teaching choral and orchestral classes at the Swindon College. His first production in October 1932 was 'The Legend of the Tsar Saltan' by Nikolai Rimsky-Korsakov, a colour-filled piece seldom seen in London, let alone in a provincial railway town. His next opera was 'Sadko' by the same composer, followed by Alexander Borodin's 'Prince Igor'. Then come three more Rimsky Korsakovs: 'Mlada', 'Ivan the Terrible' and 'The Snow Maiden'. Where else outside Russia could you have seen a Rimsky cycle in the 1930s? Swindon

The GWR/Mechanics' Institute musicians, famed for local appearances including band concerts at the Institute. Courtesy of Steam museum

The theatre prior to the 1930 fire. Note that the chairs were removable for other functions and the scenery was moved in and out on wheels. Courtesy of Steam museum

had become the epicentre for an underrated composer of quiet influence, most decisively on Igor Stravinsky.

The singers in these productions were local amateurs; Mrs Muriel Fairclough gets a credit in minor roles and costumes and scenery were handmade by society members. By 1939 the Society was booming. Its list of patrons had grown from one page to three, and the booklet was thick with consumer advertising. Frederick Ashton and Constant Lambert came from London's Sadlers Wells Opera to see Massenet's Cinderella in Swindon, the final opera before the war. Opera resumed in Swindon in 1946 with Borodin's 'Prince Igor' and an augmented orchestra. A revival of 'Mlada' was reviewed by The Times, which belatedly acknowledged that Swindon was now 'the place to look' for Russian opera.

In 1948 Fairclough put on at the MI an English folk opera, 'Hugh the Drover', by Ralph Vaughan Williams. The grand old man of English music had been born in nearby Down Ampney and he turned up at the premiere, took a bow with the cast and became a patron of the Society. In the same year, Swindon received a grant from the Arts Council of Great Britain recognising that Harry Stanley Fairclough had become an engine of national policy in musical production. Swindon's Festival of Britain opera, 'The Travelling Companion' by C. V. Stanford, was praised by *The Times*. It was succeeded by a rare staging of 'Goyescas' by the Spanish composer Enrique Granados, together with one of the first performances anywhere in the world of Kurt Weill's naive American singspiel, 'Down in the Valley'. Following his death in 1965, Harry Stanley Fairclough's memorial concert in St Luke's church in Swindon featured a performance of the 'Fauré Requiem'.

Why Swindon opera had to end can only be conjectured. It may be that the cushion of an Arts Council grant caused the society to collapse on its withdrawal, or possibly that the conductor's energies were sapped by illness. Or perhaps the times had changed and people were no longer prepared to spend evenings singing in a chorus and sewing costumes. They sat now in cinemas and coffee bars, absorbing the new and more commercial popular culture of the 1960s. As so often in the country's cultural history, the energy and determination of one person was at the centre of success - and that person was Fairclough.

The MI's Role in Saving Locomotive Building in Swindon

Between 1847 and 1855, the GWR was badly affected by the national recession and, because business recovery was slow, shareholders were becoming nervous. In 1866 following a banking collapse, the GWR company was itself virtually bankrupt. Had it lost its Swindon Works, the broad gauge trains manufactured in Swindon for the GWR's lines could not have been serviced. Morale was low, travel and trade was depressed and the limited number of skilled men the railway had employed were drifting back from whence they came. However, fortunately for the company and the town, the Swindon factory workers took matters into their own hands. They were encouraged by the appointment in 1850 of the 28-year-old Minard Christian Rea as Works Superintendent to replace Archibald Sturrock. Rea was a protege and friend of Gooch and, in a short seven year tenure, he had ushered in a new approach to company-employee relations. Rea was a key player in the New Swindon Improvement Company which raised funds and secured land for the new MI building. A culture of support and improvement was promoted through the MI that slowly turned around the company's fortunes. Rea was chairman of the Improvement Company and also vice-chairman of the MI. Looking at this historical record, Trevor Cockbill concluded that Rea influenced the MI through his strong personal and organisational skills. This effectively saved the Swindon factory from closure by stemming the haemorrhage of skilled and experienced workers. It is quite possible that locomotive building in Swindon would not have survived without the combination of Rea's drive and ideas and the MI as the fulcrum for collectivism and progressive thinking. Without this, Swindon would have become a very different place.

The Swindon Mechanics' Institute in 2024, after four decades of neglect. Photograph by Philip Garrahan

5
Alfred Williams and the Spirit of Swindon
by Graham Carter

Introduction

If Swindon had a motto, it would be 'We can do anything', since it turns seemingly ordinary folk into visionaries. It has a spirit that fosters various other positive qualities, not least an exceptional open-mindedness and tolerance of new ideas and new people. One of its manifestations is an ambition to innovate and improve – to better both oneself and one's community. Each chapter of this book contains examples of the Spirit of Swindon in action. In the history of the Mechanics' Institute and the GWR Medical Fund we find groundbreaking movements that emerged from nothing in almost no time, and in Harold Dearden and Swindon-born railwaymen-cum-artists Leslie Cole and Hubert Cook, the spirit emerges as the ambition to create worthwhile art from the least encouraging of nurseries: a town built on heavy industry.

And – as this chapter will investigate – although the Spirit of Swindon is more difficult to identify in Alfred Williams, he is arguably the greatest example of it. To attempt any study of Williams is to try to unravel an enigma, and although this chapter will consider him in only one context, as an observer of Swindon at a specific point in its history, a consideration of his wider life and extraordinary career through a brief biography is useful.

Alfred Williams' Background

Although often remembered as the 'Hammerman Poet', Alfred Williams was about much more than verse, and is perhaps a perfect example of what we may call a polymath. He was certainly an autodidact, too. But it is not sufficient to point out merely that he was self-made; such was

Alfred Williams. Courtesy of Swindon Central Library

the humility of his origins and the extraordinary depth and breadth of his eventual self-education that one might rather claim that he is self-improvement personified.

Born in 1877 at South Marston, a sleepy village four miles from Swindon, he was one of eight children brought up by a single (abandoned) mother, and left school at the age of 11 with only the most rudimentary of educations; even the morsels he had learned in school he later rejected as being largely worthless. But while his simple upbringing and limited school education might have left him indifferent to learning, he became a most passionate advocate of its power.

After briefly dabbling as a (self-taught) amateur artist and undertaking correspondence courses and private study in maths, literature and the Classics, Williams eventually found he had a gift for languages and taught himself four. This latterly included Sanskrit, which has the reputation of being particularly difficult, with native English speakers under the further disadvantage that it does not use Western characters. And yet he mastered it sufficiently for his book of translations (*Tales from the Panchatantra*) to persuade the Oxford bookshop pioneer Basil Blackwell to publish it, and it became a school textbook.

Despite Williams' humble origins, poor education and lowly social status, during his lifetime he published six books of poetry and three delightful books of prose based on local villages; there are several more works so far unpublished. All this would be testament enough to his extraordinary intellect and talent, but it is all the more remarkable that most of his works were produced while he was simultaneously holding down a five-and-a-half-days-a-week job as a steam hammer operator, in atrocious conditions and often in poor health.

Despite multiple health issues that eventually forced him to retire from the Works on medical advice, he went on to serve his country for three years in the First World War, eventually being posted to India. On his return, he and his wife built themselves a new home - literally, with their bare hands.

For good measure, he is also renowned as one of the foremost collectors and preservers of English folk song lyrics, a self-appointed project that he achieved by covering astounding distances on a basic bicycle over two harsh winters.

And we only now come to his ultimate masterpiece and most important legacy: a priceless record of industrial working conditions in the years leading up to the First World War, and arguably the most important document in Swindon's history. *Life in a Railway Factory* was written in 1911, while he was still employed by the GWR, but not published until 1915, a year after he resigned from the Works. He features here, in these pages, because he is a remarkable product of Swindon – more extraordinary, even, than the engines the town is famous for – but also because *Life in a Railway Factory* (along with what is effectively its companion, *A Wiltshire Village*) provides a priceless insight into conditions in the Works.

The GWR Steam Hammer Shop. Courtesy of Swindon Central Library.

A Manufacturing Life

ALTHOUGH IT IS a rare firsthand contemporary account of conditions in any British factory, thus giving it national importance, he wasn't the only local man who felt compelled to record the scene. As we shall see in this chapter, before him Richard Jefferies gave us a shorter account from the point of view of a visitor (rather than a worker), while afterwards, at least two Swindon artists (as featured elsewhere in this book) tried to capture what they saw and experienced through drawings and paintings. Williams almost seemed to anticipate this in one passage in his book, which is about the night shift:

It is a weird living picture, stern and realistic, such as no painter could faithfully reproduce… The faces and fronts of the smiths and forgers, as they stand at the fires or stoop over the metal, are brilliantly lit up – yellow and orange. Here are the piles of finished forgings and stampings upon the ground – white, yellow, bright red, dull red, and almost black hot; the long tongues of the fire leap up from the coke forges, and every now and then a livid sheet of flame bursts out from the stamper's dies. There is plenty of colour, as well as animation, in the picture, which obtains greater intensity through contrast with the blackness outside. (Williams, 1912, 217-218)

Williams' descriptions are always vivid and impressive, but that is not to say we can use him as a mirror. Rather, he is a window. As much as he may seem to embody Swindon ambition, vision and achievement, he was an outsider and an outlier – geographically, intellectually, philosophically, personally, and in other respects too. He even tells us (in *A Wiltshire Village*),

I have toiled and groaned long years at the furnace and steam-hammer, in the midst of ten thousand workmen; but though in it, I was never of it, and, try as I will, I cannot find many good words to say for the manufacturing life. (Williams, 1912, vii)

By any means, Alfred Williams was not your typical railwayman, and he cannot even be compared to those other intellectual, insightful and highly skilled people who built the pioneering social frameworks admired in this book. Although he saw his workmates as comrades, and sympathised with the vast majority of the workforce, he undoubtedly stood separate from them, and often quite aloof. He is a one-off.

After *Life in a Railway Factory* was published and the GWR took exception to his warts-and-all (albeit honest) account of what life was really like in the factory, one of their insinuations was that he was an inveterate country boy at heart, and this had somehow poisoned him against the harsh realities of life in the factory. A country boy he certainly was, and a champion of simple village life and country folk he was proud to be, but he was progressive and perceptive enough to marvel at technology and crave enlightenment far beyond the simple ambitions of his fellow villagers. He was not against modernism or progress itself; Alfred Williams was no Luddite. In short, he is as honest an observer as he was gifted, and we may put the highest value on his brilliant descriptions of life in the factory and beyond its walls. And when he gives us his heartfelt and deeply considered opinions on what he experienced while working there, we are bound to listen.

The first thing that must be said about Life in a Railway Factory is that while it stands as an important historical document, and that is the most obvious reason for studying it, it is as masterful a piece of writing as one could hope to find in non-fiction, and more captivating than all but the pinnacle of fictional literature. Always fluid and fluent, forever charming and often exquisite, all of Williams' prose shows him to be a natural-born wordsmith, able to produce eminently readable work, and apparently effortlessly – and all of it turned out at great speed. Furthermore, it has stood the test of time as much as any great work of its era, remaining immensely accessible, and appearing to even the 21st century reader as if it were written yesterday.

His most profound talent is as an observer of mundane scenes, and especially the people that populate them; the humbler the better. His biographer, Leonard Clark, who isn't the most generous of critics, nevertheless said he had 'a genius at describing ordinary people. His characters are as frankly drawn as any in Shakespeare or Dickens.' (Clark, 60) It would be hard to disagree.

One of the best showcases of all these abilities is Chapter VI of *Life in a Railway Factory*, where he tells us of the 'waggon smithy', reputedly the longest forge in England, which had hearths for a hundred smiths. If one only has the time and inclination to read just one chapter, this should be it. His description of the place, of the work, and especially of the men who worked there is as evocative as any poetry. He describes vividly the effect on all human senses and sensibilities, and as alien as the scene might be to us today, the reader is there with him. And if one wants to summarise the book or find a microcosm of the nature of the Works and the characters in it, you will find it in the story of the highly skilled and hardworking smiths. Williams cannot contain his admiration and respect for these men, describing them as if they are classical heroes. But he also highlights their everyday human qualities, their strengths and their weaknesses, and marvels that some of them are so resilient that they are still working in this harsh industrial crucible at the age of seventy.

It is in this chapter that he best emphasises that whatever failings the Works had, it was not for the want of hard work or commitment of the men; they (nor he) complained about hard physical labour. On the contrary, Williams strongly subscribes to it as character-building and beneficial to the worker. A 'good sweating', he says, benefits not only the body but also the mind, and – although he doesn't use the word expressly – even one's soul. It gives the smiths and their fellow railwaymen nobility.

> A delightful feeling is experienced after a good sweating at work. Every nerve and tissue seems to be aglow with intensest life; the blood courses through the body and limbs freely and vigorously, and produces a sense of unspeakable physical pleasure. Sweating as the result of physical exercise has a powerful effect upon the mind, as well as upon the body; it clears the vision and invigorates the brain, and is a perfect medicine for many ailments, both mental and physical. If many of the languid and indolent, who never do any work or indulge in sturdy exercise, were suddenly to rouse themselves up and do sufficient physical labour, either for themselves or someone else, to procure a good sweating at least twice a week, they would feel immeasurably better for it. Life would have a new meaning for them. They would eat better, rest better and sleep better. They would feel fresher and stronger, altogether more active and vigorous, more sympathetic and satisfied. Though he is, as a rule, quite unaware of it, the workman derives considerably more physical pleasure from life than do those persons, mistakenly envied, who do nothing, for everything has a relish for him, while to the others all is flat and insipid. (Williams, 1915, 94-95)

However, it comes at a price, especially when compared with agricultural labour:

> The sweat of the open fields is clean and sweet, yielded naturally; that of the other place, before the furnace, is wrung from your very heart and soul in anguish, leaving you faint, weary, powerless, and exhausted. (Williams, 1912, 105)

By contrasting the honesty of the smiths with multiple examples of the rank dishonesty common among foremen, Williams leaves us in no doubt that – for all its faults – the factory was a place of much honour, where honest labourers did an honest day's work and are therefore worthy of everyone's respect. One might expect to deduce from this that Swindon railwaymen were inspired by their work, and shared Williams' appetite for self-improvement and enlightenment, and that they reflected the positive forces that characterised the birth and progress of the Mechanics' Institute and the GWR Medical Fund. But this is not so.

Town and Country

Indeed, Williams was at pains, throughout *Life in a Railway Factory* (and periodically in *A Wiltshire Village*, too), to inform us of the broken spirit of the town dweller in general, and Swindon railwaymen in particular. And for what, compared with rural life?

A smoky and smutty gentility, a house in a drab side-street, the superficiality of the town, a weary body, a crushed and subdued spirit, a bleeding heart, or a dead soul! In the one case is natural life; in the other a forced existence. The one loves his work and runs to it of his own accord; the other hates it with all his power, and is dragged, compelled to it. (Williams, 1915, 54-55)

At this point it is useful to remind ourselves of the alternative impression provided by that other celebrated local writer, Richard Jefferies (1848-1887), whom Williams greatly admired. He gave us an altogether different picture following a visit to the Works in 1875 – two years before Williams was born. This was originally published as a magazine article called 'The Story of Swindon':

Of the men themselves, the majority are intelligent, contrasting strongly with the agricultural poor around them, and not a few are well educated and thoughtful. This gleaning of intellectual men are full of social life, or, rather, of an interest in the problems of social existence. They eagerly discuss the claims of religion versus the allegations of secularism; they are shrewd to detect the weak points of an argument; they lean, in fact, towards an eclecticism: they select the most rational part of every theory. They are full of information on every subject – information obtained not only from newspapers, books, conversation, and lectures, but from travel, for most have at least been over the greater part of England. They are probably higher in their intellectual life than a large proportion of the so-called middle classes. One is, indeed, tempted to declare, after considering the energy with which they enter on all questions, that this class of educated mechanics forms in reality the protoplasm, or living matter, out of which modern society is evolved. The great and well-supplied reading-room of the Mechanics' Institute is always full of readers; the library, now an extensive one, is constantly in use. Where one book is read in agricultural districts, fifty are read in the vicinity of the factory. Social questions of marriage, of religion, of politics, sanitary science, are for ever on the simmer among these men. It would almost seem as if the hammer, the lathe, and the drill would one day bring forth a creed of its own. A characteristic of all classes of these workmen is their demand for meat, of which great quantities are consumed. Nor do they stay at meat alone, but revel in fish and other luxuries at times, though the champagne of the miner is not known here. Notwithstanding the number of public-houses, it is a remarkable fact that there is very little drunkenness in proportion to the population, few crimes of violence, and, what is more singular still, and has been often remarked, very little immorality. Where there are some hundreds, perhaps thousands, of young uneducated girls, without work to occupy their time, there must of course exist a certain amount of lax conduct; but never, or extremely rarely, does a girl apply to the magistrates for an affiliation order, while from agricultural parishes such applications are common. The number of absolutely immoral women openly practising infamy is also remarkably small. There was a time when the workmen at this factory enjoyed an unpleasant notoriety for mischief and drunkenness, but that time has passed away, a most marked improvement having taken place in the last few years. (Jefferies, 129-131)

This is as great a tribute as you may find to the achievements of New Swindon as a community from the 1840s onwards It shows how the town's pioneering spirit was still alive and well, three decades after the Works first opened. Yet, forty years further on, Williams' impression is almost the exact opposite. He reports that the workers' thirst for knowledge and enlightenment had all but evaporated, and they appeared rudderless and leaderless:

Agricultural communities do not want education, however much they may need it. Neither do the towns want it, though they need it worse than ever, to counterbalance the artificiality of the life and environment. There are reading-rooms and other facilities in almost every village nowadays, but no one attends them… And though you have libraries and institutions in the towns, they are not utilized by anything like a satisfactory proportion of the people. Vast sums are spent upon buildings and salaries, but desperate efforts have to be made to secure the attendance of students; you have to beg and pray them to come. (Williams, 1912, 299-301)

He tells us that even the smith, who finishes work 'feeling fit and on excellent terms with himself and others' is not moved to take advantage of the library, nor anything else that Swindon can offer him in terms of education or leisure. Instead – and far from being invigorated by hard work, as previously suggested – we discover the smiths exhausted, and trying to recuperate: 'Their Sundays appear to be spent chiefly at home in rest and quietness, in company with their wives and family.' Some of them, he tells us, 'may be seen in the evening walking out towards the fields. The majority, however, stay indoors and recuperate for the coming week's work, or merely go to see their friends who live a few streets away.' (Williams, 1915, 95-97)

This somewhat explodes the idea – which is often assumed when we look back to the town's industrial origins – that the Mechanics' Institute was a perpetual magnet for the majority of Swindon railwayman. By 1915 it might still have been leading Swindon's workhorses to water, but Williams is adamant that few of them can now be persuaded to drink. When he switches his focus to white collar workers, we find a similar lack of appetite for personal improvement:

> Very few clerks, in spite of their leisure and opportunities, are bookish or endowed with a taste for literature; out of over a thousand at the factory less than twenty are connected with the Literary Society at the Works' Institute. The students and premiums have their debating classes on matters connected with engineering. They meet and read papers on technical subjects, but have little interest in anything natural or spirituel. (Williams, 1915, 135)

And just in case the reader has any doubts about Swindon's broken spirit at this time, the smiths' chapter even sets us straight on the subject of the Works hooter. In modern times, this has come to symbolise the town's lost heritage and past glory, becoming a primary source of nostalgia to the point where it might even be imagined that it breathed the very Spirit of Swindon. Not for Williams, who tells us: 'the dreaded hooter bellows out, like the knell of doom to a great many.' (Williams, 1915, 125)

So what had happened in the four decades between Jefferies' detection of a Swindon Spirit in even perfunctory workmen, and Williams' failure to find it in even the most admirable of honest workers? Before we consider the answer, we should note that even if a desire for self-improvement was now lacking, a keen community spirit still remained in Swindon, if the smiths were any measure:

> A proof of their utter good-nature and kindness to their fellows may be seen in the fact of their having, for the last twenty years, made a voluntary weekly offering of a halfpenny per man to the local Cottage Hospital. This is taken once a fortnight, the condition being that it must be unsolicited and a straight gift... This is quite independent of the annual collections made for charities, in which the smiths again always head the list by a large margin. (Williams, 1915, 97)

This reference to its hospital is one of very few mentions of either the Medical Fund or the Mechanics' Institute in the whole of *Life in a Railway Factory*. If Williams had been impressed with the social advancement and the vision of those who had built either the Works or New Swindon – both the company and the organisations founded by the men – he does not mention it in his books. It is as if the achievements of earlier generations had been forgotten or – even worse – become irrelevant.

Piece-working

THE PRIME REASON that he gives for this decline and fall of the Spirit of Swindon is the core theme of *Life in a Railway Factory*. It is written in every chapter, our guide pointing out, time and time again, how the replacement of flat basic salaries with piece work – paying men for meeting production targets, which were always harsh and often unrealistic – had been a grave error for industry in general, and Swindon in particular.

In the ever-expanding Works, an economist might argue that piecework or a similar tight system of control was a necessity or at least a partially justifiable expedient. After all, in the years that had elapsed since Jefferies' observations, the number of men working 'inside' had mushroomed from around 3,000 to between 10,000 and 12,000. A three- or four-fold increase in the workforce must have presented an enormous organisational, logistical and managerial challenge.

In itself, piecework would not necessarily have been detrimental to working conditions and wages; in theory it may even have improved the Swindon railwayman's wages and standard of living. But Williams recognised that such a system stands or falls according to the efficiency and the reasonableness of the foremen who administer it – and sadly they were neither efficient nor reasonable.

He provides numerous examples of why the foremen were, in fact, the embodiment of the harsh system they meted out; they are untrustworthy, narrow-minded, small-minded, vindictive, conniving, hypocritical, selfish, dishonest, uncaring to the point of inhumanity, inept, incompetent, ignorant, stupid and jealous; they are every inch the cowardly bully. Even worse: they bring out the worst characteristics in the men they manage. Worst of all: the foremen deliberately played men against men until they turned on each other. Those who got on best or received the best treatment by the foremen were those who were prepared to 'toady' to him and win his favour by whatever means necessary, while anyone deserving of promotion or showing initiative was victimised as the foreman protected his own position.

> Where a workman is known to possess any intellectual abilities above those commonly found and has the courage to raise his voice in any matter or to

interest himself in things pertaining to the town, or if he has in any way access to the ear of the public, he is certain to be marked for it; at the first convenient opportunity he will be shifted off the premises. Every workman who desires to improve himself in any direction other than in that which tends to promote the interests of the company is looked upon with suspicion; he is immediately included in the number of "undesirables". (Williams, 1915, 289)

He is able to draw on his own personal, bitter experience:

The steady persistence of my efforts towards self-improvement was not appreciated. Day after day the foreman of the shed came or sent someone with oil or grease to obliterate the few words of Latin or Greek which I had chalked upon the back of the sooty furnace in order to memorise them. Even my toolboxes and cupboard, always considered more or less private and sacred, were periodically smeared with fat and the operation was often carried out in a very offensive manner… At one time he had caused the furnace back to be tarred. Before the tar had completely dried I innocently chalked upon it several words that figured in my studies for the day. By the next morning the characters had become permanent. (Williams, 1915, 289-90)

And he had the last word – quite literally - when he finally resigned from the Works, in the summer of 1914 (a matter of days before the outbreak of the First World War). He famously wrote the single word 'Vici' on the iron plate on the front of the furnace: 'I have conquered.' In reality, he probably had not conquered, but at least he had escaped; that, in itself, was a rare victory. A recurring theme of *Life in a Railway Factory* is how the men were, indeed, unable or unwilling to escape. For many, the only escape was death or the workhouse:

For many enter the workhouse doors willingly, without any reluctance at all. For them it is simply an escape from the onerous responsibilities of life, from the necessity of having to toil hard to procure a living. Henceforth they are free, secure, and satisfied… and a short residence there soon brings about a spirit of total acquiescence… There is quite a crowd here from the neighbouring town – cast-offs from the factory and others – ruined in health, and otherwise unfit for service; it is a striking testimony to the efficacy of modern industrial and urban conditions in producing physical wrecks and paupers. The majority of these are young men between thirty and forty. (Williams, 1912, 97)

Invariably, whenever any history references Swindon Railway Works, the men are said to have worked 'inside', the apprentices having 'done their time'. They were contemporary colloquial terms, and in modern usage they often generate some humour, as if the factory was some kind of prison. But it was a prison to Williams, and he makes several references to the Works in those terms.

> While the men are inside the walls of the factory, they are under the most severe laws and restrictions, many of which are utterly ridiculous, and out of all reason considering the general circumstances of the toil and the conditions in vogue; they are indeed prisoners in every sense of the term. (Williams, 1915, 305)

Urban Life

They are partly ensnared by the superior wages compared with agricultural counterparts, even though they are lower than rates paid to equivalent workers in other industries. But what Williams particularly laments is how the workers, as he sees it, have been seduced by the trappings of modern industrial capitalist life; it has turned them into materialists, especially compared with their country cousins.

> The hardships of the industrial life are far greater than those of the village… everything is sacrificed for a few more shillings in wages. If the dweller on the land knew to what extent he must eventually suffer, he would never be so anxious to get away into the town; by the time he has made the experiment and finally learned for himself, it is too late for repentance. (Williams, 1912, ix)

After the piecework system, this pursuit of the trappings of modern life is Williams' secondary explanation for Swindon's disastrous decline, and he gives numerous examples. Some are amusements and entertainments provided by the Mechanics' Institute, as if it (and therefore the town's railwaymen and families) had become not beneficiaries of its success, but victims. Ironically, Jefferies had also accused ordinary workers of this same 'imprudence', but added that it was virtually their only shortcoming; Williams is much more specific and indignant, leaving us in no doubt about what he thought passed for frivolous and fatuous in Swindon at this time:

> I am not yet become the apostle of absolute modernness for its own sake. Do you think we are happier to-day, in our brick-and-tile houses, stuffed up with gaudy furniture and trappings, baked with the heat in summer and half-

frozen with the cold and draught in winter, highly rated and rented, forced to work hard and live hard with a hand-to-mouth existence to pay for the luxury of fine rooms, wall-paper with dado, a smoky or sultry kitchen-range, glass doors, and artificial tiled floors and pavements? Are we better for all the increased comforts and advantages of the newer dwellings and manner of living – the fine upholstered suites and sideboard, American organ or piano, imitation pile carpets, lamps with brazen fittings hanging from the ceiling and in the hall, pictures and overmantels, which must find a place in the majority of houses to-day? Do you imagine for a moment that we really benefit by the greater facilities we have for indulging the natural propensity for exciting amusement and enjoyment – dancing and music, roller-skating, billiards, whist-driving, the theatre, cinematograph, the tramway, and the football field? Are we better in body, warmer, healthier, stronger, more comfortable, happier, wiser, in any respect whatever, by reason of the fastidious and fantastical modes of dress which have crept in upon us; the ever-changing styles of headgear imposed upon a simple and foolish people by a crafty and gluttonous ring of manufacturers, fashion-mongers, and tradespeople; the high, choking collars and skittish tie; swagger-cut jackets with padded shoulders; brightly coloured waistcoat with fancy buttons; trousers with tight, close-fitting legs, made to turn up at the bottoms; button boots of brown calf or kid, daintily made, and pointed at the toes; silk handkerchief protruding from the top pocket; gold or silver ring on the finger; and a large cane or stick like a shepherd's crook in the hand? No wonder so many hundreds of workmen are pale, and white, and haggard-looking, creeping backwards and forwards to the shed like whipped curs, bound hand and foot, body and soul enslaved to the hard task, forced to work as many hours as they possibly can to pay for it all, and in debt at the end, the very slaves and subjects of their employers at all times – hopeless, helpless, soulless and spiritless. (Williams, 1912, 17-19)

Although the piecework system had actually made them poorer, it had still robbed them of the will to escape or better themselves, and many paid for this with their health, while some paid with their lives. Their illnesses often turned fatal, while the poor conditions also often led to debilitating injuries and sometimes death as the result of accidents. Williams put the cause of many of these down to the men prioritising the chasing of targets above personal safety. Another effect was the general oppression of life in the Works, which caused them to fall into a kind of stupor, and this inattention inevitably brought catastrophic consequences amid the hot metal and the general chaos and confusion of the factory environment.

> The noises of the steam and machinery drown everything else. You see the workmen standing or stooping, pulling, tugging, heaving, dragging to and fro, or staggering about as though they were intoxicated.

On the night shift it is even worse:

> Everything is swinging and whirling round, and you seem to be whirled round with it, with not a thought of yourself, who you are, where you are, or what you are doing, but keep toiling mechanically away. Ofttimes you would be quite lost, but the revolutions of the machine, the automatic strokes of the hammer, and the habit of the job control you.

And:

> The eyes ache, the ears ache, the teeth ache, the temples ache, the shoulders ache, the arms ache, the legs ache, the feet ache, and the heart aches. I have many times wishes, in those dark, awful hours, that the hammer would smash my head; that I might be suddenly caught and hurled into eternity, and I have heard others express the same wish openly and sincerely. (Williams, 1915, 217-219)

The situation that industrial workers found themselves in at this point in history might go a long way to explaining why so many working class men were so eager to sign up to serve in the First World War. It is said that many volunteered because of the prospect of adventure, but in the pages of *Life in a Railway Factory*, one finds evidence that another driving force was the opportunity to escape from harsh factory conditions. Writing in 1911 (before signing up for the war provided this new means of escape), Williams could not hide his disappointment at his comrades' unwillingness to find a way out, and how this demonstrated not only a loss of spirit, but also of pride and self-respect.

> Once a man becomes settled in the factory he is very reluctant to leave it. Notwithstanding the rigour of the system imposed, he usually remains there till the end of his working days, unless he happens to meet with an accident or dismissal. He soon loses his self-confidence and independent spirit. The world is considerably narrowed down in his view; he feels bound to the life with indissoluble fetters. (Williams, 1915, 297)

This failing is not to be found in their rural counterparts:

> Village folk never were so generally abject and slavishly obedient to every precept and nod of the 'maaster" as is usually represented; it is an insult to the rustic population ever to suggest it. (Williams, 1912, 21)

Here we should pause to understand that despite the dark satanic impression of the factory he conveys to us, Williams is neither a cynic nor a fatalist. Nor is he a fantasist, although some have been tempted to interpret his deep fondness for the pastoral life in his works as evidence of this. His nostalgia for village life is even evident in the early chapters of *Life in a Railway Factory*, where he tells us of isolated oases of natural flora and fauna within the walls of the Works, and pines for Liddington Hill, which may be glimpsed in the distance from certain corners of the gigantic site.

While accepting that this kind of idyll is almost impossible to find in the town itself, he argues that workers might at least seek it out in their spare time. They could do this by taking trips into the countryside, and he notes that this is not an uncommon occurrence for some, while they also relish opportunities to travel further afield.

> Every hour spent outside the factory walls is a precious addition to life; whoever willingly throws away the opportunity of enjoying it is guilty of the highest folly and negligence. He is the curtailer of his dearest rights and liberties, the forger of fetters for himself and his children after him, and the sooner the working classes can be brought to see this the better it will be for them. (Williams, 1915, 295)

And perhaps there is hope for them, after all:

> The privilege of a quarter-fare for travel, granted by the railway companies to their employees, is valued and appreciated, and widely patronised. By means of this very many have trips and become acquainted with the world who would otherwise be unable to do so. (Williams, 1915, 246)

Later chapters also talk of a growing trend in society in favour of 'going back to the land', and although Williams welcomes this he doubts that his fellow workers have the will left to achieve it. Neither do they have aspirations to escape inside their heads through intellectual pursuits. He notes that there was little appetite for such things as art and literature in Swindon.

Politics, religion, the fates of empires and governments, the interest of life and death itself must yield to the supreme fascination and excitement of football. There is almost total lack of spontaneous interest in anything – with the exception of sport and politics – that happens in the world without the factory walls and the immediate vicinity of the town. The great business of life is entirely ignored; small inclination is discoverable – even if there were opportunities – to pay attention to anything but the ordinary duties and routine of the shed… The men of the shed are always eager to listen to and take part in political discussions, but they are, as a rule, totally indifferent to the interest of literature… As for general culture, it may at once be said that the educated man is not wanted at the factory.(Williams, 1915, 287-289)

While Williams is in agreement with some of the sympathies of the labour movement of the time, he strongly disagrees with the aims of trade unions during this period. The strongest measure of his views on such matters can be found, ironically, in his portrait of rural life, *A Wiltshire Village*, which is another illuminating, worthwhile and gratifying read. There can be no sweeter, more enjoyable, more heartfelt record of rural and village life in the 19 and early 20 century than this; it is another masterpiece.

The Spirit of Swindon Reborn

A WILTSHIRE VILLAGE is a close companion to the railway book, having been written a few months afterwards (although published three years sooner). It argues for a return to rural values and lifestyles by contrasting life in South Marston with life in Swindon, and noting how the rise of the town had been in direct proportion to the decline of rural communities. Part of the problem, he admits, is the general industrialisation of Britain and the migration of agricultural folk, right across the whole country, to fill industrial opportunities, lured by higher wages; and Swindon is the prime example.

Higher wages there may be, and slightly shorter hours, and a few other "privileges" – a bigger house to live in, perhaps, with more games and amusements, but they can never compensate one for the unnatural confinement in the smoke, and stench, and gloom, week after week, and year after year; for the fever and the fret, and heart-gripings, wasting health, the sense of despair and utter helplessness that grows upon the individual there; and, above all, the loss to character, of sound healthy principles, hardihood, the power to battle with life and circumstance, and that jewel, so easily lost and hardly recovered – simplicity of taste, thought, method, and objective. (Williams, 1912, viii)

He reiterates, several times, that the pursuit of higher wages is misplaced, telling us: 'All the wages in the world will not compensate a man for the loss of his own happiness and inner peace of mind,' (Williams, 1912, 54) and adding:

> The aim of the working class should be not altogether for the highest wages, which must often be procured with terrific effort, but for more leisure, more rest, more time for study and thought, more time to live; a greater freedom, good health, a clear conception of themselves and things, and a truer sense of the real independence of it. (Williams, 1912, x)

But all is not lost; Williams is hopeful (although not anticipating) that Swindon railwaymen might find a way out of their prison, and is eager to add that it had not always been like this and remedies were available. However, it required both the men and the company and its officials to jointly choose a different way forward.

> A decade and a half ago one could come to the shed fearlessly, and with perfect complacence; work was a pleasure in comparison with what it is now. It was not that the toil was easy, though, as a matter of fact, it was not so exhausting as it is at present, but there was an entirely different feeling prevalent. The workman was not watched and timed at every little operation, and he knew that as the job had been one day so it would be the next. Now, however, every day brings fresh troubles from some quarter or other. The supervisory staff has been doubled or trebled, and they must do something to justify their existence. (Williams, 1915, 304)

This is a crucial statement. It tells us that life in the railway factory, and in the little houses in its shadow, had once been bearable, and that the Spirit of Swindon had produced a life that even Williams, the dyed-in-the-wool son of the village, could find palatable. It also tells us what might be achieved if only employer and employee would work together. This is key because it reminds us that however much the success of Swindon's fledgling industrial society and the ongoing success of its social frameworks might be attributed to either the benevolence of the company or the vision of its employees, in reality, neither can claim the credit. What made it possible was a partnership between the two, based on a mature, mutual understanding of each other's needs.

We may turn to Richard Jefferies once again, and his aforementioned essay on Swindon, as evidence that this co-operation was still present in 1875. Although not named here, his reference is clearly to the extraordinary insight and paternalism of Joseph Armstrong, the Chief Mechanical Engineer at Swindon from 1864 to 1877 (the year of Williams' birth), for whom the workforce demonstrated genuine affection:

Gunner williams. Courtesy of Swindon Central Library..

> This small nation of workers, this army of the hammer, lathe, and drill, affords matter for deep meditation in its sociological aspect. Though so numerous that no one of them (sic) can be personally acquainted with more than a fractional part, yet there is a strong esprit de corps, a spirit that ascends to the highest among them; for it is well known that the chief manager has a genuine feeling of almost fatherly affection for these his men, and will on no account let them suffer, and will, if possible, obtain for them every advantage. (Jefferies, 129)

Whether Williams got his wish and the Works and the town recovered to emulate its past glories requires a lengthy study. Leonard Clark pointed out that the piecework system was still in place in 1939, when he started to compile Williams' biography, nine years after his death, but we might conclude that the foremen nevertheless got their comeuppance. By the start of the Second World War, the GWR had risen from the apparent crisis witnessed by Williams before the First World War to experience what was surely its heyday in the 1920s and into the 1930s. This is the era when the Swindon-built Castle and King Class locomotives became arguably the greatest of all steam locomotives – and all while the rest of the world was buckling under the Great Depression and spiralling towards another world war.

This would surely not have been possible if the same conditions that Williams observed in 1911 had continued, when he was able to provide numerous examples of why the system was hopelessly inefficient and grossly wasteful.

Perhaps there is a clue, too, in the reaction of Felix Pole to *Life in a Railway Factory*. A highly respected figure in industry – he was knighted in 1924 – Pole was the General Manager of the GWR between 1921 and 1929, exactly the period that is considered Swindon's heyday. Although the GWR's dismay at the contents of Williams' book is often quoted, this is far from the impact it had on Pole, who was impressed. 'In praising the book,' said Leonard Clark, 'he said that the Swindon conditions were well known to exist by the Paddington staff, and could well be improved were it not for the attitude of certain high officials. He begged Williams to call on him if he was ever in London. Williams... considered this a most unusual honour.' Clark, 90)

And so he might; Pole was not only a fellow Wiltshireman, who was born in the same year as Williams (1877), but grew up in an agricultural community, and began his career at Swindon in the same year as Williams (1891), as a lowly Swindon telegraph clerk. He could not have failed to recognise the parallels, nor what an extraordinary character he was, giving us hope that Williams' book had some influence on him, and that it was at least partly responsible for a change of strategy by the GWR after the First World War.

What we can be sure of is that while Williams noted a severe decline in Swindon, compared with the origins of the new town in the 1840s and through the time of Jefferies' scrutiny, its fortunes would be transformed again. The Spirit of Swindon was, at some point, reborn. Its leaders became inventive, open and resilient enough to navigate the decline of the railways over several decades while new industries were established. Meanwhile, some of those past glories, like the establishment of the Mechanics' Institute, would be echoed in, for example, Swindon becoming the first town in the country to open a dedicated arts centre in 1946.

Conclusion

THE QUESTION THAT remains for us is whether Williams' remarkable impact on the world was despite Swindon's effect on him, or whether it might have been because of it? Is there a case for proclaiming him a product of the Spirit of Swindon, and might we even take the even bolder step of nominating him as its prime example?

Alfred and Mary Williams. Courtesy of Swindon Central Library

We have already seen that he was an enigma, an outsider and doggedly single-minded – simply different to all Swindonians, before or since. And no one could pretend that he had any more affection for Swindon than for the age of capitalism and materialism he found himself reluctantly born into. However, it is difficult to imagine how this aspiring wordsmith would have found his voice or left us any legacy if he had remained in South Marston.

His original inspiration was his mother; she gave him his thirst for knowledge. But otherwise there is nothing in his fond endorsements of rural life and his affection for his home village to suggest it would have encouraged any of its inhabitants – not even him – to aspire to become a man of letters, let alone to have his works published.

In Swindon, on the other hand, the people he came into contact with must have provided something of an example, and while he was proud to be affiliated with his fellow villagers in South Marston, it was in Swindon that he found his best friends and (with the exception of his wife, Mary) his greatest supporters. He lacked any financial gain from his books, but the reliable, regular and comparatively good income he obtained from working for the GWR in Swindon allowed him to effectively subsidise his ambition to publish books. It is therefore difficult to imagine how he could ever have achieved this on the meagre income of a seasonal agricultural labourer, had he had continued to work on the land. We should also point out that his greatest legacy, *Life in a Railway Factory*, would also, of course, have been impossible if he had never worked there. Although his works afford virtually no recognition to the Mechanics' Institute, the GWR Medical Fund or the successful community that grew up around it in Swindon, he would have been fully aware of the story of those who built it, and it is difficult to conceive of a man as astute as Alfred Williams not drawing some inspiration from all of that.

One thing is certain: that Alfred Williams would not have appreciated any call for Swindonians to claim him as one of our own, but we shall do it anyway. Because the more one learns of him, the more extraordinary a figure he becomes, until one becomes bold enough to suggest that if there is a Spirit of Swindon, Alfred Williams was - and is - the embodiment of it.

References

Clark, Leonard 1969. *Alfred Williams His Life and Work*, David & Charles.
Jefferies, Richard 1909. *The Hills and the Vale*, Duckworth & Co.
Williams, Alfred 1912. *A Wiltshire Village*, Duckworth & Co.
Williams, Alfred 1915. *Life in a Railway Factory*, Duckworth & Co.

6
The Swindon School of Art - picking up steam
by Philip Dearden

Introduction

Throughout the nineteenth century, a limited elementary education was often thought to be sufficient. Many educational transformations followed, and this chapter is about one of these: the early development of Swindon's School of Art, with particular reference to its leadership under Harold Dearden between 1920-1950. The complex roots of education and training in England are examined in the context of the nineteenth century Arts and Manufacturing movement. The Mechanics' Institute (MI) played an early role in Swindon, preceding the various forces for the delivery of a centralised national Art and Design curriculum. The Art School and the arts in Swindon were very much 'picking up steam' in the inter-war years: - the formation of the Swindon Artist's Society, an Arts Discussion Group and the Swindon Sketch Club all helped raise the profile of the visual arts in Swindon and subsequent establishment of the Swindon Art Gallery. The growth of the Swindon School of Art from its nineteenth century roots can be linked to a local story and then a national and an international one. At first the battle was to obtain any access to education and many educational institutions sought the highest status available. Apparent local successes and setbacks were often overwhelmed by unexpected national and international forces.

The Swindon School of Art was fashioned by several powerful themes that preceded any institutions or buildings in the town. The first was the struggle to develop universal education – first at elementary level, then at secondary and technical level and at higher level. The second was the ongoing debate over the purpose of education and the extent to which it is limited by the requirement of a workforce to be educated and trained for economic competitiveness. The third theme is the growing role of the State in education and training provision and the fourth the growth of professionalisation and formal qualifications for individuals in the labour market. These common international themes are joined by a fifth rooted in the particular social conditions of England, namely the continuing role of social inequality and social class. Most societies are affected by social division but its strength in England has been a constant presence in the development of the education system. As Tawney famously wrote in 1931, 'The hereditary curse upon English education is its organisation upon the lines of social class'.

For much of the twentieth century secondary and technical education was divided by class, sex, school/college and function. Today this is still a factor and debates concerning primary, secondary and technical education have been joined by another about who can access higher education and what type of higher education they need. Here we look at aspects of this ongoing development in relation to the Swindon Art School - from the nineteenth century until the 1960s.

Art Applied to Manufacturing - Key Forces behind the School of Art.

THE FIRST TANGIBLE force behind the School of Art was the MI movement, which had its own historic roots in Scotland. This movement played a key role in the thinking and development behind Swindon's own MI at the heart of its railway village. It is important to note that the MI which opened in Swindon in 1843 offered a range of early art classes to its members. This was half a century before the School of Art in Swindon and the North Wiltshire Technical School were established in 1896.

Other powerful forces included the deliberations about the nature and purpose of art and design education which were prominent in the second half of the eighteenth century with the involvement of bodies such as the Royal Society for the encouragement of Arts, Manufactures and Commerce (RSA). Established in 1754, the RSA held its first exhibition of contemporary art in 1760 and the first industrial exhibition in 1761. The impact of manufacturing at scale became important in the face of increased competition from Europe in the early decades of the nineteenth century. Attention moved from the technical to the aesthetic quality of British manufactured products and debates about art and design increased in the 1830s.

In 1835-36 a Select Committee of the House of Commons was set up dominated by the followers of the philosopher Jeremy Bentham and economic liberals. The aim was to find a way to improve design and to help industry work better while supporting the development of 'taste' in a society where the middle classes had cultural aspirations for themselves and others. George Wallis was the Deputy Commissioner for the highly successful Great Exhibition in 1851 and he argued that Art and Design Schools would go one step better, since 'the primary purpose is to teach art as applied to the manufacture'.

By the 1870s there were over 100 provincial schools of Art and Design in England. Their development seems precocious compared with other parts of the nineteenth century education system. However, they arose for specific and economic and social reasons. In the workshops and factories self-taught workmen and women could copy and make, but did not necessarily have the skills to design and create the new styles needed in an expanding market.

The curricula taught at the Swindon MI and the Art School were all influenced by these early forces. In the early days they were in line with the centralised compulsory art curriculum devised by Sir Henry Cole. As the central Victorian figure in British art and design education between 1852 and 1873, he directed a department of Government disseminating standards in design by means of compulsory education. He instigated the first national system of compulsory art and design education justified primarily on the grounds of social (in Victorian times synonymous with commercial) significance. Uniform standards of design and craft workmanship were introduced in place of regional peculiarities, so that the typical qualities of goods made in Britain would be recognisable in all markets of the world.

Cole's centralised art education system introduced in 1855 was micromanaged from his 'headquarters' in South Kensington (now the Victoria and Albert Museum). This was known as 'the terminus' and Britain's art education was run on a 'uniform gauge' with colleges located on 'branch lines'. (One of Cole's early crusades had indeed been on behalf of a uniform gauge for the railways). A key driver in this system was the method of paying art teachers according to the results their students gained in a national competition. This was judged by 'headquarters' and its purpose was to ensure the compliance of art teachers across the country.

In time the South Kensington System, as it became known, would be exported to the empire, to Canada and the USA. It consisted of gradated stages of competence. Elementary school pupils aged 5-13 with artistic talent were recognised with scholarships which could be for several years' education in a technical or art school. A smaller number of successful students could win further scholarships towards certified distinction and perhaps become a qualified teacher in Art and Design.

Cole's highly prescriptive Art and Design Education system focussed unrepentantly on drawing and had no less than 23 stages and 57 separate parts. The aim of the system was not to try to nurture great artists but 'to provide education to the eye and the hand, such as would enable the common workman to follow his trade with more exactness and precision'. Pupils were taught the smallest of details, such as how to follow the outline of an image provided on an authorised instruction sheet. Outline geometry was taught alongside linear perspective and pupils copied rigid forms from standard flat reproductions, often spending many months on these tasks. At an advanced level, only the most competent were considered able enough to do work which was called 'Design' work.

The effects of Cole's system persisted in some respects until as recently as 1965, when the art school qualification known as the National Diploma in Design was discontinued. This was so styled in spite of the fact that some thirty percent of those who gained it were fine artists, and thus were still respecting Cole's principle that at its most proficient all creative work was designing.

The Beginnings of Adult Technical Education

THE ROOTS OF the Swindon Art School rose from attempts to create a basis of adult technical education in England in the first part of the nineteenth century. The people involved believed that not only should there be a basic education but some wider possibility of higher learning beyond 11 or 12 years old. The most radical believed that alongside political and economic rights were educational rights. The Chartist and working-class reformer William Lovett argued,

> Possessors of great wealth still consider education their own prerogative, or a boon to be sparingly conferred upon the multitude instead of a universal entitlement for the advancing of man and the gladdening of his existence.

Such ideas of a universal entitlement fed into the MI movement which was constituted of an uneasy combination of self-help and reform from above.

The MI movement for the education of the working classes began in Scotland in the 1820s. Once the many benefits of education for working men became clear, MIs spread rapidly. So successful was the movement that by the end of the 1820s there were at least twenty-four Institutes around Scotland alone, and a number also in America, Canada, and Australia. The first English

MI was formed in London in 1823 (becoming the basis for Birkbeck College). MIs on the pattern of the Birkbeck model followed in Bristol, Manchester, Liverpool, Sheffield and Leeds and others followed in virtually every large town or city in England. Within the Institutes a development pattern of educational activities was often followed. Whenever buildings could be made available, libraries were established with reading rooms and other rooms for lectures and educational classes. Evening classes in literacy and mathematics were common, with institutes near large engineering establishments offering tuition in machine drawing and the theory and practice of mechanics and workshop technology.

These early initiatives sometimes struggled because they were founded in the middle of a period of economic and social turmoil. Many workers lacked the basic literacy to participate and education in night schools had to compete with other demands - work, family and social activity. Middle class support was influenced by self-interest too, with even those involved often being wary that education might undermine existing society. Many were either hostile or simply indifferent. Despite the many challenges, by 1826 over a hundred MIs had been founded and by 1851 as many as 700. By 1900 there were over nine thousand MIs worldwide.

While some people thought that educating the working classes would lead to anarchy and revolution, many believed in the importance of 'levelling-up' society. Although formed by and for men, women were allowed to attend lectures and some lecture programmes were provided separately for them. The legacy of the MIs philosophy, based on the idea of good education for all, is still strong in some quarters. The MI movement is judged a success for providing a firm foundation on which further education was established by the beginning of the twentieth century.

Although some argue that the MI movement initially failed to support adult working-class education, its ultimate success was due to the flexibility of the MIs responding to the local needs of industry. (Dohmen) The Great Exhibition of 1851 had shocked government into the need to support industrial development in the face of foreign competition. This led to the 1889 Technical Instruction Acts which brought many MIs into what was effectively state ownership. The committees of MIs developed models of education and training delivery that many Colleges of Further Education have continued to follow until this day. To be successful, they introduced a range of courses for adults, at both elementary and advanced level, and qualifications which supported local employer needs. They thus made a crucial contribution to industrialisation and the workplace.

Many MIs eventually went on to become Colleges and Universities, or libraries and community halls. Others were repurposed as hotels or offices or were demolished. Many Colleges of Further Education and some universities (e.g. Liverpool John Moores University and the University of Wolverhampton) can trace their origins back to their local MIs.

The Swindon MI and the provision of Art Classes 1843 - 1896

DANIEL GOOCH'S DIARY covering the time he spent in the Dundee foundry in 1835 records, 'There was a very good MI here, of which I was a member and attended the lectures regularly. The library was also a good one for such purposes.' With his early positive experiences of the MI in Dundee, Gooch led the GWR in Swindon as an enthusiast and keen supporter for the establishment of a local MI.

The Swindon MI was established in 1843 as an organisation 'for the purpose of disseminating useful knowledge and encouraging rational amusement'. In the same year, a library began in Swindon set up by the first generation of Great Western Railway (GWR) workers with Daniel Gooch as its first president. There were fifteen founder members, and the library then held about 130 books. On account of the fact that so many local people had access, it is considered one of the first public libraries - not just in Britain but in the world. Technically it was established as a private collection because it was owned and run by the GWR worker. The vast majority of Swindon workers were GWR staff and, since their families also enjoyed the benefit of everything the MI did, most of the local population could borrow books. Members kept their own catalogues at home from which they selected the books they wanted to borrow and these were regularly updated. An influx of new people to Swindon during the Second World War highlighted the fact that those without railway connections in Swindon had fallen behind the rest of the country when it came to the provision of libraries. In 1943 - exactly a century after the GWR workers first considered the idea of lending and borrowing books - Swindon finally got its first official public library. This was an example of the GWR dominance reducing as the local economy grew and diversified in the post-war period.

The foundation stone for the MI building was laid by Lord Methuen in 1854 (see illustration on page 54 above). This gave rise to the popular misconception that it started as a result of the GWR's benevolent disposition towards its employees. However, it was the Swindon people, encouraged by a few forward-thinking men within the community, who built the MI for themselves, not the GWR. Paid for via subscription by the GWR workers in Swindon Railway, the building was designed and constructed by Edward Roberts. Formally opened in May 1855, the Swindon MI building was where it all happened. It had lecture and reading rooms, a dining hall, bathing facilities and initially an adjoining market. It was the physical focus and educational and social heart of the railway town. It was enlarged in 1892-93 to a design by Brightwen Binyon, after which the committee opened its health services to other local workers. Trevor Cockbill strongly believed that Swindon's was unique amongst the MIs. He maintained that it was 'the place where the respectable and socially aspiring could be and needed to be seen'.

In effect the governing Council of the Mechanics became the governing body of the new town in Swindon, and the Institute quickly became a vital part of the growing community - a place where people could both enjoy themselves and generally improve their lives. However, while the MI catered for the educational needs of local people, it was not a training school. It did, however, stamp its mark on the educational and cultural development of the town. In addition, it importantly, helped lay the foundations and beginnings of the new Swindon and North Wiltshire Technical Institute.

The teaching of Arts in the Swindon MI

IN THE 1880s the Education Board Committee of the Swindon MI was providing adult Art Classes along with Science and Technical classes. Lectures were held in the theatre on a wide range of subjects especially science and engineering by lecturers visiting from across the country. In 1887 there were large numbers of students studying 'Freehand and Model Drawing' and 'Geometry and Perspective' and 'Geometry'. These subjects were taught by a team of seven local staff many of whom were employed in the Swindon Works and were led by Mr W. Board of the Stroud School of Art.

The art classes were taught in a variety of locations across town and not just in the MI building. For example, in 1893 there were 215 art students who attended classes held in College Street Board School. These classes covered Second Grade Freehand and Model Drawing, Perspective and Third Grade Drawing, and Shading from Models and Casts. In the same year 31 students attended evening art classes and a further 31 attended afternoon classes that were all held in the Town Hall. A further 31 attended Painting Classes (Oils and Watercolours) held at College Street Board School. Mr Broad, the Head Art Teacher, was to persevere for many years ending his service in 1899. During his long tenure he oversaw some very significant institutional developments related to the teaching of art in Swindon.

A GWR Magazine article of November 1890 about the distribution of annual prizes presents some interesting figures and thinking regarding the students attending educational classes and the nature of some of the subjects they studied, such as art drawing. In his Prize Giving speech Viscount Cobham refers to the subject of Art. He notes that he could understand why some people might be tempted to state that, 'railways are strictly utilitarian things' and thus ask, 'What have railways to do with art?' He then emphasises GWR thinking, 'that when building railways, bridges, locomotives and carriages it was the duty of their manufactures and handicraftsmen, if they could do so without the sacrifice of economy strength or durability, to make things as beautiful as they possibly could'.

In 1889 the Technical Instruction Act placed technical instruction outside secondary schools and passed responsibility to the new County Council and County Boroughs and their Technical Instruction Committees. The new act also allowed the new committees to levy rates in order to raise the standard of art and science education for artisans and as a consequence ally themselves more closely to local industry through education. A new level of education was formalised, and technical schools/colleges were introduced.

In 1891 a Technical Instruction Committee was formed in Swindon representing the Local Boards, the School Board, the MI, and the Wiltshire County Council. An open town meeting was held, and it was agreed to raise a loan in aid of the construction of suitable buildings for the accommodation of the Swindon and North Wiltshire Technical School. The MI Council then reported, 'The Council of the Institute have transferred to this Technical Institution Committee, the management of the Classes, which have for many years past been carried out by the MI'.

Swindon and North Wiltshire Technical Institute - the Development of Swindon Art School 1897-1914

CONSTRUCTION ON THE three-storey Swindon and North Wiltshire Technical Institute on Victoria Road started in 1894 on land donated by Major W. V. Rolleston. It was made possible by grants from the Department of Science and Art and the County Council. It was built by Messrs Long and Sons of Bath, to a design by the architect and surveyor Thomas Ball Silcock (1854-1924). The rather magnificent Flemish Baroque style three-story building cost £14,000 with an additional £15,000 spent on extensions and equipment. The School of Art which was on the top floor of the building was the first purpose-built School of Art in the Southwest. As noted by Ranald Lawrence, Victorian

The Swindon Art School, part of the Technical Institute (later called the College), Victoria Road. Local Studies Unit, Swindon Central Library

art school architecture embraced the functional requirement for the provision of plentiful light and air. At the same time it satisfied the formal expression for a new kind of public building supported by local rates and properly fit for its place in the civic heart of the town/city.

The building was formally opened on 27 January 1897 as the Swindon and North Wiltshire Technical Institute. The GWR Magazine reported on the formal opening event as 'a red-letter day.' Lord Herschell presided over the opening and spoke about foreign competition in the technical arts. He carefully noted that Britain was falling behind its German neighbours because they had devoted, care, attention, money and energy to technical and scientific education. He went on to say that whilst many in industry complained that they did not see immediate results for all this technical training, there could be no doubt 'that training of the eye and hand and resonating processes which came from technical and scientific teaching was of incalculable importance to those who are going to fight the industrial battle of the world'. Herschell's speech was well received and in responding, Lord Fitzmaurice moved 'that this meeting ... expresses its satisfaction at the completion of the new technical school and the progress made towards the establishment of a complete system of technical instruction in the town and district.' It was indeed a momentous and significant moment in the progress of Swindon's educational system as well as in the provision of training for those who were now being prepared for the twentieth century as opposed to the nineteenth.

With the 1902 Education Act (the Balfour Act), the MI relinquished control of the Swindon and North Wiltshire Technical Institute. This was because the Education Board was abolished, with the Borough Council's new Education Committee taking over instead. Nevertheless, several key members of the GWR were elected to the new committee and the college retained strong links with the GWR. The 1902 Act resulted in another significant shift in the direction of art teaching. It started to phase out the Department of Science and Art's Payment by Results Scheme. This meant that payments to Schools of Art were largely conditioned by student successes in public examinations and the National Competition for Schools of Art. Inside the Art School located on the third floor of the Technical Institute, students sat at desks in silence drawing models, statues and busts or copying template exemplars from the National Art School in South Kensington, adhering to Cole's tightly structured national curricula described above. In its early years the Swindon Art School had a high turnover of Principals and Art Teachers. Many of them were well qualified, having themselves studied at the Royal College of Art (RCA) formerly the School of Design in London with its highly prescriptive practices.

When the School of Design opened, it had declared its 'special object' as the training of art teachers, designers for fabrics and art workmen, for craftsmen, not 'painters of easel pictures.' At this time a clear distinction was established between the 'higher' discipline of teaching drawing to serve the needs of manufacturing, and the 'lower' discipline of art for the purpose of encouraging creativity. (Souleles) This distinction was to play out in action in the newly established Swindon Art School. Between 1901 and 1906 Mr Clarence Mawson ARCA, was Head Art Master, assisted by three female teachers. At this time some of the applied arts were transferred to the engineering and commerce departments leaving the full-time art staff to concentrate on 'fine art'.

Records of art student numbers for each year are not always available but, from 1903 to 1905 these varied between 27 and 51. The new Art School was clearly struggling with low student numbers. In 1906, the year Mr W Parkinson ARCA was appointed Head Art Master, the Art School was again reorganised, and its staff further reduced. In that year a total of 63 students enrolled for Day Technical and Art Classes. This figure rose to 78 in the following year. In 1908 it was reported that,

> From the time of the opening of the school it has been found that doubtless on account of the absence of a specific artistic industry in the district the demand

for pure Art Instruction (as distinct from Art Instruction which forms part of other curricula) has been small….(but)… the Committee have now appointed a fully qualified Art Mistress, who has been trained at the Royal College of Art, to the second post in the Art Department'.

In 1909 Mr J. S Vickers ARCA was appointed alongside Miss C. E Horner AMC. They worked together and taught a small number of art students for the next four years. In 1913, Mr E.E. Anderson was appointed Head Art Master. He specialised in Marine Painting and in that year the enrolment total in the Art School was 59, but only four of these were full time students with the remainder studying part-time or evenings only.

In July 1914 few people had any idea of the scale of the catastrophe that was about to occur and in a few months the world was engulfed in war. Of six million UK volunteers, or conscripts, one in eight were killed and one in four wounded. The War took away a generation and stopped the possibility for education for many. Mr Anderson's stay in Swindon was short lived. He left Swindon during the war in 1915, taking up the post of Head of Art at Winchester College. Not surprisingly, art student numbers in Swindon continued to fall during the war. Likewise, the length of the Art School Annual Reports also fell, from 40 pages in 1915 to just 3 pages in 1919.

A stained-glass window in the Technical School was dedicated to the forty-four of its students who were lost in the war. The window shows a boy in school uniform holding the Union Jack with an angel behind and the symbols of learning at his feet, with above and below the words 'Greater Love Hath No Man Than This - 1914 In

Stained Glass Window Photo by Peter Benson. Commemorating past students who gave their lives during the Great War 1914-1918.

Memoriam 1918'. The lower part of the window carries the names of former pupils who lost their lives during the First World War. In 2010 the window was successfully moved to the new Swindon College campus in North Star Avenue. It is now on display in the college's learning resource centre.

Swindon Art School in 1920 - A New Start

THE 1920S HAVE been described as a decade that demanded change, but were plagued by poverty and unemployment, social unease and industrial action. This was certainly the case in Swindon where work and life were often challenging. In 1920 Harold Dearden was appointed as Head of the Swindon Art School. On his arrival in Swindon, he found that the Art School had suffered from a lack of leadership since Mr E.E. Anderson had departed in 1915. There were only 80 students enrolled in the Art School. Moreover, many of these were part-time students attending evening classes. Only 17 students were enrolled for painting courses. Building on his experience gained from training at the Art School in Rochdale and the Royal College of Art (RCA) in London, plus his teaching experience in the School of Art and Crafts in York, Halifax Art School and the Gloucestershire College of Art and Design, Dearden quickly set about changing things. Under his leadership there was a quick upswing in the teaching of fine art, especially drawing and painting.

Copies of the Arts School Prospectuses and Annual Reports of the Technical Institute/College provide a good record of the growth in number of the art school students in the following years. There is also documentary evidence about how Dearden developed the Art School. For example, over the next few years Art School students began exhibiting their artwork in the Annual Wiltshire Arts and Craft Exhibition, a prestigious local event. The profile of the Art School was quickly on the rise. Dearden and his small team of two staff quickly set about establishing some clear and ambitious objectives. These were developed and set out in the annual Arts School prospectus and became progressively more ambitious over the decade. They carefully balanced national policy priorities with local needs and also provided a range of qualifications which gave art students professional credibility.

In 1930, the School of Art was providing Drawing, Painting, Design, Modelling and Craftwork adapted to the requirements of various types of students. These included, 'those who wish to become Professional Artists, Architects or Designers of Posters, Book Illustrations and Advertisements, Stained Glass etc. Industrial workers and craftsmen who desire to supplement the training received by them in various workshops. Students who desire to make their general education more complete by the study of Decorative and Pictorial Art and cultivation of refined taste. Students who wish to become Teachers of Art.'

Students were prepared for the Board of Examinations in Art, the National Skills Academy for Manufacturing (NSAM), Examinations for Teachers in Elementary and Preparatory Schools, for the City and Guilds of London Institute Examinations in Painting and Decorating, Handicraft Embroidery, and so on. A career as an art teacher depended on first obtaining a school certificate as proof of a good general education.

There are also clearly documented examples of Dearden working collaboratively with his Art School students. In 1924, he was commissioned to make two large (133 x 183cm) oil on canvas paintings for display at the Swindon Civic Offices. These were inspired by the town's motto of 'Salubritas et Industria'. While Dearden designed the two pictures, they were painted with assistance from his art school students whose collaboration was key.

The two paintings were hung in the Town Hall for many years, but after the second World War they were taken down. In 1984 they were rescued from a skip, having sat under a pile of rubbish in the Civic Offices for many years. Their discovery baffled the Arts Officers of the time but an article in the Swindon Advertiser confirmed their identity. A former Art School student and successful local sculptor, Carleton Attwood, identified them and solved the riddle set by the Swindon Advertiser. The 30th of January 1984 edition of the Swindon Advertiser stated that the Thamesdown Council planned to restore the pictures and hoped to hang them in the Mechanics Institute once it was repaired. Sadly, some forty years later this has not yet happened.

Harold Dearden moved to Swindon with an established track record as an artist. He was a prolific painter in oils, watercolours, monochrome sketches, pencil, chalk, charcoal and pastel. The facilities and equipment in the Art School aided his work and his new Swindon environment presented him with an interesting new range of industrial and social subject matter. Several of his early pictures capture the heavy manual labouring work that went on in the town.

Dearden became active across the town collaborating with others as the importance of art was slowly becoming more recognised. In 1927 the GWR, which still had a good working relationship with the Art School, inaugurated an Annual Exhibition of Arts and Crafts which was open to all its employees. It did this through its Social and Educational Union. The earliest exhibition events were all held at Paddington in London, however several Swindon Railwaymen who were studying part time at the Art School exhibited there.

Salubritas (Health) by Harold Dearden 1924, Oil on canvas, 133 x 183cm Courtesy of Museum and Art Swindon, SWIMG:PCF2

Industria (Industry) by Harold Dearden 1924, Oil on canvas 136 x 182.5cm Courtesy of Museum and Art Swindon, SWIMG:PCF1

In 1926 the Swindon and North Wiltshire Technical Institute was reorganised and the growing importance of art was recognised alongside other technical subjects. The three Schools of Engineering, Commerce and Art were given equal status within the newly named Swindon Technical College.

The expansion of the Art School continued and by 1928 there were 142 Arts students, with Dearden assisted by three full-time and four part-time staff. In 1928 the Art School students held an exhibition of their own work in Swindon and this was a significant development for both the Art School and the town. In 1929 there were 208 Art students enrolled at the Art School and Dearden had recruited a team of ten well qualified teaching staff. By 1930 a wide variety of subjects were taught to both part-time and full-time students who could be enrolled on several courses. The two-year Intermediate Art and Craft courses included Life and Costume Drawing, Anatomy, Figure Composition, Modelling, Architectural Drafting, Principles of Art and General Knowledge and Creative Design for a Craft. The three- or four-year National Diploma in Design included specialised instructions for the National Diploma in one or more of Painting and Drapery, Mural Design, Dress Design, Embroidery, Leatherwork, Lettering and Illumination; and Wood Engraving and Lithography. The wide variety of subjects and increased student numbers meant that teaching rooms and resources were stretched. In 1930 the teaching timetable needed to be extended until 9pm on weekday evenings.

One of Dearden's key roles was to mentor and coach young students, several of whom became well established artists including Leslie Cole and Hubert Cook (see chapter 7). In 1932, students in the School of Art achieved national recognition by making successful submissions of their work to the Royal Institute of British Architects and the Royal Academy. The sculptor, Harry Carleton Attwood studied art and wood carving between 1924-1930 at the Art School. Despite winning many awards at the Art School he agonisingly failed by half-a-mark to gain a scholarship in sculpture at the Royal College of Art. However, he made a reputation with much admired works such as the busts of Reuben George and Alfred Wallace. Some of his other well-known public commissions are 'Golden Lion' in Regent Street in Swindon and 'The Watchers' at Toothill Village Centre.

In 1934, Dearden formed the Swindon Artists' Society arguing that 'there was need for better exhibition facilities than the Swindon Art School could provide'. Working with Mayor W. E Bickham OBE, the Council Chambers in the Town Hall were used for the first and successful Swindon Artist's Society Annual Art Exhibition. Between 1934 -1939 the Society experienced slow but

Workmen by Harold Dearden c.1920s, oil on canvas, 20 x 22.5 cm. Private collection.

steady growth. Further annual exhibitions were held in various local premises, including a school room behind Regent Street, the derelict building of the old GWR hospital and the foyer of the then public library in front of the town hall. Life for artists in Swindon was not always easy but their dedication, coupled with the support from the Swindon Artists' Society, ensured that the best of their artworks were put into an annual exhibition for the public to view and sometimes purchase.

The Second World War Period 1939 - 1945

IN ANTICIPATION OF war, workmen in Swindon were working sixteen hours a day putting up air raid shelters across the town. At the same time trains full of evacuees were pouring into the town, packed with unaccompanied children or mothers and babies from London. More than 4,000 refugees and evacuees arrived for the relatively safer shelter provided by Swindon. By the end of the first month of war local emergency services were on the alert and the slogan 'Swindon will be ready' was intended to reassure, but cast an ominous light on what might be in store for the town. Frequent air raid alerts, severe rationing and scarcities of everyday necessities ensured that the period of the war was a miserable time for many across the country. Although the Swindon sirens sounded often, the town escaped the devastation that was wreaked on other towns and cities in the southwest including Bath and Bristol. However, by the end of the war, in May 1945, some 104 bombs had fallen on Swindon with 48 people killed and 105 injured. Around 50 homes were destroyed and 1852 damaged to some degree. Despite the serious challenges of the war, the annual cycle of art students entering and studying at the Art School continued during the war period. The teaching of courses continued, albeit with fewer staff and topics being taught. Resources in all areas of college work were often in short supply, and in the town basic foodstuffs were sometimes short as circumstances worsened.

The Swindon Art Discussion Group

BUILDING UPON THE success and popularity of the Swindon Artists Society, a Swindon Art Discussion Group was formed by Harold Dearden in 1940. This quickly flourished with dozens of people attending lively discussions and debates on a wide range of art topics. A number of Swindon Art School students attended the sessions, but membership of the discussion group was from across Swindon and nearby areas. An interesting range of visiting speakers attended and presented, and a wide and rather eclectic range of topics were discussed and debated. Of great interest is that the early Art Discussion sessions were held during the war. It could be that during the long dark days of the war some Swindonians simply wanted to elevate their thinking and consider other things for a while. Maybe discussing aspects of art helped them cope with the horrors being reported by the media and going on around them.

As later noted by Harold Jolliffe, Swindon's first Borough Librarian and director of Swindon's first Art Centre,

> The various art exhibitions held in Swindon were a great asset to the Arts Discussion Group who found much to praise and criticise in the fare offered. It was a most exhilarating experience to be one of a group of ninety people assembled to discuss modern French art and moreover in the middle of a war!

After the war the Swindon Art Discussion group continued to grow and it helped raise the profile of visual art across the town. As an occasional

Wet Evening or Rainy Day, Regents Circus, Swindon by Harold Dearden c. 1945. Oil on canvas, 90 x 90.5 cm. Courtesy of Museum and Art Swindon SWIMG:2018.66

plein-air artist himself, Dearden encouraged all his students studying fine art and drawing at the Art School to go sketching out of doors. With the possible influence of Thomas Ablett, Harold Dearden was motivated by a wish to eliminate drudgery from the drawing classroom and to restore a 'lost delight' in picture making. Like Ablett he saw young people not as future artisans in some predetermined scheme for industry, but as individuals who would make more vital contributions to the community if their observational and retentive faculties were fully developed. In 1933 he formally established a Student Sketch Club within the Art School. He had often encouraged a number of others across Swindon, especially those in the Swindon Artists Society to go sketching outdoors. By 1949 this activity appealed to a dozen or so hardy adult members of Swindon Artist Society who joined forces with some of the Art

Waiting for the Train by Harold Dearden. Oil on canvas 75 x 91.5 cm. Courtesy of Museum and Art Swindon SWIMG:2022.13

School students in an informal way and called themselves the Swindon Sketch Club.

In the early days of the Sketch Club the restrictions on membership were as strict as those for the Swindon Artist Society. However, by 1951 the Swindon Sketch Club Annual General Meeting attracted 18 people and an outdoor exhibition of members' work raised the sum of £2 8s 4d for the Artists Benevolent Fund. This was the first of the Sketch Club outdoor exhibitions. Many others followed, including one in 1952, when this small group took their pictures to London and exhibited at Foyles. The Sketch Club continued in Swindon with active members holding regular exhibitions well into the late 1970s.

In 1920, when Harold Dearden was appointed, there were only 80 students at the Art School with many of these being in evening classes. When he retired in 1950 there were 530 art students following a wide range of qualifications and courses. In his 30 years at the Art School not only had he overseen a huge increase in the number of students and a massive expansion in the art curriculum, but also a huge increase in public interest in the arts across Swindon.

The Locarno or Corn Exchange, Harold Dearden 1947. Oil on canvas 45.5 x 61cm. Courtesy of Museum and Art Swindon, SWIMG:AG102

Speaking to an Evening Advertiser Reporter on his retirement on 20 June 1950, Harold Dearden said,

It has meant a lot of hard work, and it has been hard going. Facilities have not always been what I would have liked. Since 1947, however, the equipment

Central Library by Harold Dearden 1960. Courtesy of Museum and Art Swindon. Oil on canvas 45 x 45cm SWIMG:AG189

and staff have considerably improved. Many people do not realise what a wide variety of subjects are taught in the art department. In addition to painting, drawing, sculpture and architecture, classes range from pottery making, dress designing and dress making to cabinet making, painting, and decorating.

It was further reported that:

> One thing Mr Dearden would like to see is the development of printing in relation to book production and general commercial art. This however would necessitate more accommodation being made available at the College, where he says, the question of space has been a "nightmare". Mr Dearden feels that there is an advance in the appreciation of Art in Swindon. He also feels there is scope for further development of the Swindon School of Art.

Harold Dearden died in Swindon on the 6th July 1969, aged 81. Five years before his death he was both incredibly pleased and proud that Swindon had finally opened its first ever Art Gallery in Apsley House, a 19th-century building on the corner of Bath Road and Victoria Road in Swindon's Old Town. Not only did Swindon finally have an Art Gallery but it also had space for exhibitions put on by such groups as the Swindon Artists' Society.

Kenneth Lindley, Artist and Art Teacher in Swindon, echoed what Harold Dearden had been saying for many years. Writing to the Swindon Advertiser in 1964 he argued that the development of the arts in Swindon was not a luxury.

> 'The new Swindon Art Gallery is a splendid achievement which all concerned deserve congratulation. The arts are not, as appears to have been suggested, "the icing on the cake" to be catered for as a pleasant afterthought once such important affairs such as street lighting, sewage, youth services etc. have been provided. They are essentially the driving force of civilisation.
>
> We measure ancient civilisations not by their purely material achievements but by their achievements in music, painting, sculpture, literature and poetry. Without these things life becomes a dull monotonous progress from birth to death and unworthy of the status of humanity.
>
> Without the arts we would have no great thinkers, no dreamers of dreams or visionaries; the human race would come to a standstill, bogged down in its own materialism. Is this the kind of world we want for ourselves and our children? For too long we in Swindon have had to rely on the voluntary efforts of a few and the undeserved generosity of one far seeing and public-spirited benefactor to fill an awful cultural gap in the town.
>
> Now that we have a gallery worthy of the best exhibitions and an Art School which can give impetus to the practice of the visual arts let us be thankful and give praise where praise is due. Let us also determine that these provisions shall be the beginning, not the end of the growth of cultural facilities in our town.

Conclusion

It can now be seen that several themes and powerful forces fashioned the early teaching of art subjects in the MI and later in the purpose-built, prestigious Swindon Art School. There were impressive developments by the turn of the century, but then the First World War took a heavy toll. As a result, the progress of teaching in the Art School was somewhat derailed.

The appointment of Harold Dearden in 1920 led to a resurgence of the teaching of art and a growing interest in the arts in Swindon. Despite the economic and social challenges of the 1920s and 1930s, Dearden soon had things back on track and the arts were again picking up steam. Indeed, the head of steam built up in the interwar period was so strong that the teaching of the arts, and the developing arts culture in Swindon, proved to be resilient to the ravages of the Second World War.

It is concluded that the development of the Swindon School of Art, the Swindon Arts Society, the Swindon Sketch Club, the Swindon Art Discussion Group, and ultimately the Swindon Art Gallery, have all led to the sustainability of a strong arts culture in the town. Collectively these Swindonian institutions and organisations have led to some great artists and artwork being Made in Swindon.

References

Cockbill, Trevor 1991. *Our Swindon, when summer suns were glowing.* (The Quill Press Swindon)

Dohmen, Renate 2020. 'Art Industry, and the Laws of Nature: The South Kensington Method Revisited', *Open Arts Journal* Issue 9.

Grinsell, L.V., H.B. Wells, H.S. Tallamy, John Betjeman 1950. *Studies in the History of Swindon* (Swindon Borough Council)

Jolliffe, Harold 1968. *Art Centre Adventure* (Swindon Borough Council)

LSU Local Studies Collection, Swindon Central Library

Souleles, N. 2013. The Evolution of Art Design Pedagogies in England: Influences of the Past, Challenges for the future. *The International Journal of Art & Design Education (iJADE)*, Special Issue: Design Education: International Perspectives and Debates, Volume 32, Issue 2, 243-255

WSHC Wiltshire and Swindon History Centre, Chippenham.

7
The Worker as Artist: Creativity in a Company Town
by Philip Garrahan

Introduction

STEAM TRAINS PROVIDE the prevailing image of interwar Swindon and with good reason, since this was the place where they were manufactured by the Great Western Railway (GWR). The town and the company served each other - although not necessarily in equal measure - and the outside observer might have been forgiven for thinking they were one and the same thing. This symbiotic relationship thrived for a century after the GWR first came to Swindon in 1841. As the town grew from its origins as a small rural community, few things happened there that were not related directly or indirectly to the company's dominant economic and social influence. The GWR's corporate reach extended far beyond the workplace, influencing culture, education, health, housing and social life - as evidenced by the chapters in this book. While many of these contributions to the book have assessed the significance of various agencies and structures in a company town, the focus can now turn to Swindon's artistic life.

The premise of this chapter is that art is the deposit of a social relationship. (Baxandall) On the one hand there are the artists, and on the other their teachers, financial backers and others who supported their creative work. They do not operate in isolation, but are situated in a specific and - as this book has argued - exceptional social context. Key questions that can be addressed are: how did railway factory workers become artists in the first place; what do they tell us about working and social life; and how was their work received when exhibited for public viewing? The history of Swindon's art thus opens a potentially insightful window on the past. The role of art as social documentary is central to this, as are the connections made between memories and heritage in the twenty-first century. So, the analysis of art additionally informs modern debates such as those about safe working conditions or the provision of a public health service. These are very broad topics for a single chapter, but they can be narrowed down by examining the work of two of Swindon's artists.

Building on the previous assessment of Harold Dearden and the School of Art, the focus here is on men who were tutored by him, Leslie Cole (1910-1976) and Hubert Cook (1901-1966). Their art adds to the growing evidence about the vitality of cultural life in Swindon around the GWR factory. It also critiques the classed nature of the art world they encountered and exposes the dangerous and harsh working conditions in the factory. Cole and Cook represent a generation of worker-artists who contributed to Swindon's thriving cultural environment in the inter-war years. Similar working-class artistic creativity has been recognised in the northeastern coalfields by the Pitmen Painters and elsewhere such as in Welsh mining communities. However, despite Swindon representing an important example for understanding the relation between art and identity in company towns, it has been largely neglected. The following sections introduce Cole and Cook's early lives in more detail by describing their artistic careers and examining a selection of their prints and paintings. It concludes with a critique of the ways in which collective memory expressed through art is deployed by the local heritage sector.

Both artists were brought up in Swindon and began their artistic careers by taking part-time classes in the evenings and at weekends. Cook had to persevere with exacting manual work in the factory for over twenty years and for much of this time juggled factory shifts with part-time learning. Both men progressed to further art study in London in the 1930s, where Cole took a full-time course. Cook also continued to study, but on day-release from working a forty-eight hour week as a machinist at the GWR Works. Sometimes showing work at the same art exhibitions, the two artists also shared a small studio during the 1930s.

Cole and Cook's experiences during the war differed, but they remained friends and often exhibited in the same art shows and competitions. Their stories are indelibly linked to being 'inside' at the GWR Works and their art is deeply influenced by the experiences of work there. After the end of WWII their paths followed similar routes as they became teachers and college lecturers living away from Swindon. Both were recognised internationally for their achievements in the lithographic printing technique and exhibited drawings, watercolours and oil paintings. Cole's work was significantly recognised by a posthumous solo exhibition at the Imperial War Museum in London in 1986, while Cook remained at the margins of the art establishment. Both men's lives were shaped by industry and war and in later life they returned to these experiences in their art.

How Cole and Cook became Artists

LESLIE COLE WAS born in 1910 in Swindon, where his father held a lower middle-class job as a clerk in the GWR Works. The family home was a substantial terraced house with gabled bay windows, two main stories and an attic room in the pitched roof. It was built at the turn of the century in a growing and prosperous area of Swindon Old Town. Between 1927-1932 he studied at the Swindon School of Art. After passing the Board of Education's Drawing and Industrial Design Examinations he trained as a teacher on a one year course at the Birmingham Central School of Arts and then worked in a school in Sutton Coldfield. In 1937 he was awarded a diploma in mural fabrication, fabric painting and lithography by the Royal College of Art. He then became an assistant lecturer at Hull College of Art where he was put in charge of lithography. In the years immediately preceding the outbreak of war, Cole had completed the transition to a professional art career and way of life.

Hubert Cook was born in 1901 in the then rural village of Wroughton near Swindon. His birth certificate shows his father working as a 'Carrier', indicating an unskilled labouring job. His family moved to Swindon where he joined the Chief Mechanical Engineer's department when he was 15. He briefly served in the Royal Flying Corps during WWI and became an apprentice shaping machinist with the GWR at the age of 17. This training lasted for five years and he was to remain with the company for another two decades before re-joining the RAF in 1942. Manual work was a choice made of necessity in Swindon, since in Cook's own words he had a living to make and a family to support. Like Cole, he studied part-time at the Swindon School of Art and also was particularly sponsored by its head, Harold Dearden. This led to the award of a scholarship for further study in London comprising course fees, a weekly day release from work and a travel pass from the GWR. When the course at the Central School of Art in London ended in 1938, Cook returned to full-time work in the steam hammer shop making dies for drop hammers.

Limited educational opportunities were available, yet these two men soon made finely executed self-portraits. These are in pencil on paper, and both are technically accomplished and done with confidence in the medium. They use close framing of the sitter with relaxed but serious gazes and are seen from similar viewpoints. They are well-dressed, with almost identical mixing of shirts and ties with pullover and formal jacket. These are not the clothes for manual factory work and the similarities indicate that the drawings were very likely studies for an art course both men were taking.

Both of the artists focussed on here are men, reflecting the exclusion of women from much employment in the railway industry in the interwar years. The GWR Works in Swindon relied mostly on men for its heavy manual labouring and women were employed there only in clerical and other support roles. Their shop floor opportunities on the manufacturing side were limited to examples such as the preparation of fabrics for coach seating and varnishing passenger carriage woodwork. There was generally more reliance on women on the factory floor during WWII, but the railway industries as with many others soon reverted to type after 1945.

Exhibitions and Recognition

BY THE MID-1930S Cole and Cook were steadily gaining recognition for their artistic work from agencies outside of Swindon. In 1934 Cole exhibited at the Senefelder Club, an international association for the promotion of lithography and he also exhibited at the Storran Gallery where works by Picasso, Sickert, Epstein, Skipping, Eurich and Dobson were also shown. Cook exhibited at the annual Senefelder show in 1937 alongside Matisse and Derain. Like Cole, his work in this medium was beginning to gain recognition and his print 'Unloading at a Railway Siding' discussed below was included in a separate exhibition of British contemporary lithographs. A copy was later bought by the Metropolitan Museum of Art in New York for its permanent collection.

This external recognition was not without its local precedent inside the company in the form of the GWR's Educational and Social Union (ESU). This organisation was one facet of the ways in which the Company had gradually extended its presence in the lives of its employees far beyond the factory gates. There were already horticultural societies, outdoor sports competitions and leagues for board and card games. A literary society had been started in 1885 and associations for amateur dramatics, singing, the scouts and so on followed. The first full length opera was performed in 1930 and Swindon became known for its various orchestras. The company's umbrella organisation for all of these social and recreational activities was the ESU, which by the time of the

Hubert cook, Self portrait

Leslie Cole, Self portrait

interwar years had four thousand members in Swindon.

Cole and Cook took advantage of the in-house opportunity to display their art through shows organised by the ESU. In a 1927 initiative to overcome the bitterness and divisions which were the legacy of the General Strike of the previous year, a revised Manifesto for the ESU was published. This aimed to bring workers and management together under a corporate mantle,

> …to banish all ill feeling and lack of harmony that have arisen recently, and to restore friendly relations between all employees. Upon these conditions depend the revival of the former social and recreative activities of the Union and the resuscitation of 'helping hand' and other movements of practical good-fellowship.

One strand of the initiatives subsequently taken by the ESU was the holding of the first annual exhibition of arts and crafts made by GWR employees and their families in 1927. A prestigious panel of judges would award prizes to the best entries. This was an immediate success and it took place every year until 1939, but was not revived after the war. In order to explain the rationale behind the proposal for the exhibition, the Manifesto asserted,

> that the welfare of the Company's employees is dependent upon, if not identical with, the prosperity of the railway, and that the most essential work of an organisation aiming to secure the well-being of the staff is the encouragement of all-round cooperative efforts to promote the Company's welfare. (ESU Manifesto)

This elision of individual identity and well-being with GWR prosperity and strategy captures the essence of corporatism: it candidly aimed to align the entire workforce and their families behind the GWR's commercial future and profitability. This was not a novel turn of events since, as other chapters in this book have shown, the GWR's version of a company town in Swindon was already socially complex and firmly embedded.

The arts and crafts exhibition provided a platform for workers and their families to share their personal creativity with a wider and more appreciative audience. The head of the ESU under whose auspices the exhibition ran was the baronet Sir W. James Thomas, a mine owner and leading capitalist. The opening ceremony was presided over by a member of the House of Lords, the Right Honourable Viscount Churchill. He was from a prominent aristocratic family and was not only chairman of the GWR from 1908 until his death in 1934, but was also connected as a director to the British East India company and the shipping line P&O. These establishment names lent approval to the event as a whole. However, it was the presence of Percy Jowett, Principal of the Central School of Art in London as chairman of the competition judges, which gave further re-assurance to any critics from the art world. The GWR exhibition thus aimed to raise the bar in relation to artistic and creative standards - this was to be much more than a provincial run of the mill arts and crafts show.

The shows were held in GWR headquarters in Paddington, with the exception of two years when building works at the station there necessitated use of another venue. The choice of Swindon as the alternative confirmed the town's importance in a network of lines and stations that stretched from London to Cornwall, South Wales, the Midlands and Merseyside via Birmingham. As well as accommodation in its hotels, the GWR could offer railway passengers onward sea passage to Ireland through connections with its own fleet of ferries. While up to fourteen thousand people worked in the Swindon Works in the interwar years, the company's total workforce including its whole rail and sea network was of course larger than this.

Artists from Swindon featured regularly in the ESU exhibition awards, none more so than Leslie Cole and Hubert Cook. The most significant of these awards were for drawing, painting and printing. The ESU exhibition catalogues reveal that between 1927-1939 Swindon was over-represented: for example, half of the entries in the prestigious oil painting section were submitted by Swindon based artists in 1930. During the late 1920s, Cook was a regular contributor along with JEC Brown and TE Summerhayes. Others from Swindon were G.A. Bailey, E. Lowe, J.E. Lockyer and George A. Reason. Cook won competition medals in drawing and oil painting and one of his entries in 1928 was a drawing of Lockyer. Both men had other entries with the same titles, namely Head of a Girl and The Artist's Wife. Cole's study of a partially nude woman used his future wife as a model and she was also depicted in a clothed portrait submitted by Cook. All of this points to a Swindon group working closely together and using themselves, and their wives, as models - presumably to save on costs. The ESU exhibition records demonstrate that the Swindon Group was unrivalled in numbers and artistic output compared to other sections of the GWR's national workforce,.

The pictures from this period analysed below come in the main from two sources: the annual ESU exhibitions of Arts and Crafts and the collection held by Museum and Art Swindon. In 1985 the museum paired Hubert Cook with Alfred Williams a local writer in a short exhibition entitled, 'A Railway Artist and a Railway Poet'. More than seventy of the eighty seven images by Cook on display were loaned by his son and widow. These privately held drawings, lithographic prints and proofs and paintings are described in various levels of detail in the guide pamphlet to the exhibition. The ESU exhibition catalogues were published annually and are more exact in image information albeit mostly lacking reproductions. The shows attracted press coverage which sometimes carried photographs of artistic works, as in the case of Cook's self-portrait discussed above.

Although the exhibition records are detailed in relation to author, media and titles very few of the originals or reproductions of them have been accessed for research purposes. Some may be in private collections or others may not have survived at all. The oil painting titles indicate conventional subjects such as landscape, portrait and still life. In the opinion of the judges, however, changes were soon afoot. The adjudicators to the 1929 exhibition in Paddington wrote that,

> There has been a new understanding of late of the value of work of a modest kind done by men and women of various occupations showing an intimate observation of the ordinary things of daily life and the moving qualities that can be associated with them'. The Company was congratulated for its, '…enlightened encouragement' of these non-professional artists, emphasising that, '…the work done for particular surroundings is invariably more successful and interesting than that which has no reference to the lives of the people that made them'. They continued, 'It was interesting to find in some cases that competitors had used the life around them as material for their pictures. This always produces work of more vitality than ideas that are second-hand. (GWR Magazine, 1929)

Several interpretations can be placed on these comments. Firstly, they might be read as generous assessments of young, creative and talented artists. They needed strong encouragement to continue with their art, given that many were also GWR factory employees doing strenuous manual work in demanding circumstances. The judges included senior figures in the art world and they could bring their expertise and experience to bear on the work presented to them in the competition. On the other hand there is an air of condescension in their words, coming as they do from members of the art establishment to which neither Cole nor Cook at the time belonged. In 1929 they were yet to study in London for formal art qualifications and their exhibition successes were still to come. They lacked the pedigree typically embraced by the art establishment: neither had been tutored by a well known artist, as Dearden himself was in the early stages of his career; nor were they members of a group of artists already recognised for its work. In these respects, it is hard to avoid the classed nature of the art world at the time which relied on education and entitlement. The ESU judges speak of 'work of a modest kind' which only sometimes goes beyond ideas that are 'second-hand'. This patronising categorisation meant that outsiders like Cole and Cook faced an uphill struggle and it is to their very great merit that they eventually overcame these obstacles.

Although Cole and Cook's early development as artists overlapped, it was Cole's professional development that produced the most immediate results. While teaching in Hull, he went to sea in a trawler converted for mine-sweeping to capture wartime scenes and he also visited other sites where military work was under way for the war effort. These inspired him to produce sufficient evidence for the War Artists Advisory Committee to gain a commission as a war artist. His nominal rank of captain opened the door for visits to several theatres of war, including Malta, Greece, Germany and the Far East.

His images of the war are sometimes routine, showing officers and men in the armed forces at war. However, his focus was also on the victims of war and his depictions of civilian life reflect a strong personal association with the suffering of people caught up in combat. Cole never shirked from portraying the suffering he encountered. In Greece in 1945, he painted the Mother Mourning the Death of a Priest which is in the Imperial War Museum. Cole powerfully shows war breaking people's lives. This was part of his engagement with the lives of ordinary people to the point of making it the hallmark of his work. He was present at the liberation of the Nazi death camp in Bergen - Belsen and of an internment camp for women in Japan, both of which he painted. (Yorke) These experiences inspired the works which the Imperial War Museum used for its 1986 exhibition called To The front Line, rendering Cole a much admired War Artist.

Although being trained in art classes to paint conventional subjects such as landscapes, portraits and still lives, Cook departed from these conventions in 1931 with his innovative 'The Night Shift - Boiler Shop'. This won an ESU competition medal and in 1932 his entry was beaten to the competition silver medal by Cole's 'Portrait of An Old Lady', which is examined below. In 1939 Cook dominated the portrait section and won three silver medals, one bronze and the Sir George Handover Trophy. His art work was interrupted by the outbreak of war, as he embarked on what turned out to be a fruitless effort to also gain a commission as an official war artist. The Swindon Evening Advertiser noted in February 1943 that he was changing his style and becoming more impressionistic: 'I'm trying to convey the impression of dirt, heat and sweat and I think I've nearly got It now'. Two months later he was reported to have achieved more recognition when his lithograph 'A Welder In a Boiler Shop' was shown at the Royal Academy. His drawing 'Steam Hammer' was shown in the 'Artists of Fame and Promise Exhibition' at the Leicester Galleries and was also written up in The Times.

Artworks

THE STANDARD ART historical approach to the visual interpretation of artworks focuses on elements such as composition, the use of different techniques to show form and depth, iconographic analysis, and figurative or impressionistic features. However, for the purposes of the following discussion the main issue of interpretation is the relevance and meaning to be attached to images that depict industrial life. Is the work showing man overcoming metal in heroic terms as the corporate propaganda of the time would have us believe? Is there an alternative view of industrial art which challenges the viewer to think critically about exploitative working conditions? And, is art from the inter-war years interpreted more positively by its contemporaries rather than by an idealising and nostalgic modern audience?

When working class art emerges and receives a wider audience, this can be mediated by the external intervention of teaching and learning in the subject. For example the academic Robert Lyon was a bourgeois mentor to the Pitmen Painters. He brought with him a command of high art and normative aesthetics that reflected the views of members of the art establishment. This raises the problematic of whether outside assistance is an essential catalyst, or does working class art have its own independent agency? Remaining true to art borne of personal experience is the special appeal of the Ashington Group of Pitmen Painters and its reputation for authenticity. Where such mediation is lacking or takes another form, as seems likely on first examination in Swindon, does the artwork differ substantially in these respects? The essential discourse between work and life, between labour and leisure can be evidenced in the experienced based art of Cole and Cook.

Working class art has an oppositional potential given the working conditions and constrained social horizons and mobility which prevailed. In such circumstances, art might challenge and perhaps unsettle conventions and norms. This can emerge from a limited goal or more universally by aiming to replace the prevailing capitalist system, its patriarchy and so on. It might stand alone as a personal statement or be incorporated in a social movement. The artist's subversive expressions may be consciously declared or be intuited by the observer. These can be defining elements, especially given the political dimensions of art in the tradition of social realism.

Several of Cole and Cook's images are set in the GWR Works foundry, where in the 1930s over 10,000 tons of metal castings in iron and in non-ferrous metals such as brass or bronze were cast. A 1935 GWR magazine article describes one of the foundry workers as 'the shingler'. He was employed in the, '… rolling mills at Swindon - believed to be the only place in the country where the ancient art of hammering white-hot iron is still practised.' (GWR Magazine, 1935) This idealised account is understandable in the context: it was published in the Company's own magazine and so did not question the hazardous and oppressive working conditions endured in the factory. These circumstances were the responsibility of the Company and any criticism of its management by an in-house own publication would have been unthinkable. We can turn to a local writer Alfred Williams for an authentic account based on his personal experience. He is principally known for his poetry, rural chronicles and preservation of local folk song lyrics, as discussed in Graham Carter's chapter in this book. His personal and decades long employment as a steam hammer operator in the Works produced this account of the shingler:

> Various prices ranging from 15s to 50s a ton are paid for shingling and forging. These depend on the weight of the piece and the degree of finish required. The shingler is clever and expert, and he is not highly paid at the works, considering his usefulness, for he is a great manufacturer. Thousands of tons of metal must pass through his hands in the course of a year, and the work is very hot and laborious. By the age of fifty the shinglers and forgemen are usually worn out and superseded at the forge. When they can no longer perform their duties at the steam-hammer they are removed from the manufacturing circle and presented with a broom, shovel, and wheel-barrow. Their wages are cut down to that of a common labourer, and thus they spend their few remaining years of service. At an early age they drop off altogether, and their places are filled by others who have gone through the same experience.

With these contrasting accounts in mind - the idealising GWR Magazine article and the intense realism of Williams, the worker/writer - we can turn to contemporary artists for their interpretation: this is done by comparing a print by Cole and a charcoal and pen drawing by Cook which both depict the shingler at work. Cole's 1939 lithographic print Men at a Steam Hammer shows a trio of shinglers and demonstrates his significant expertise in this

Three Men at a Steam Hammer by Leslie Cole 1939. Lithographic print on paper. 41 x 29cm. Courtesy of the British Council

The Iron Man/Shingler by Hubert Cook 1942. Charcoal on paper. 11 x 19cm. Courtesy of Museum and Art Swindon. SWIMG:2016.56. TEMP6

medium. It was bought by the Contemporary Art Society and is now in the Wakefield Collection held by the British Council. This atmospheric image of men working in the foundry has authenticity as well as forcefulness, with the setting cast into relative darkness by the light from the white hot metal. Sparks fly from the inferno of heat and light within, yet the workers seem unperturbed because of the normality of these circumstances for them. The central figure focusing on his task is represented realistically, but those to each side of this trinity of figures are more stylised. The man to the right appears in elongated fashion and the right hand figure is posed resting on his work tool with a seemingly incongruous expression and ready to take his turn at the steam hammer. Cole's direct knowledge of manual factory workers is evident: some tasks are more arduous and demanding than others and workers rest on the job while they can. Nevertheless, there is an overwhelming sense of men pulling together in this image and a message about teamwork and collective endeavour in factory labouring comes across clearly.

The print impresses through the figures' dominant physical presence and firm stance and fortitude in the face of demanding work. They embody the strength of labouring men in industry and so the primary motif could be assumed to be about man's mastery over metal. This was a theme common to art described as social realism that was used for ideological purposes and taken to extremes in Stalin's Soviet Union. It is no surprise in the context of corporate propaganda that the GWR magazine piece cited above focused on the 'medieval art' of shingling undertaken by the 'burly and strong' worker. But, this was at the expense of honesty about working conditions that could be often dangerous and sometimes life-threatening. A closer look at the iron boots, shabby leather aprons and primitive protection provided by gauze face-guards put this print in a different light. The workers have to rely on a crude pair of giant tongs as their only aid in manipulating the white hot metal billet across the factory floor.

A similar response is evoked by Cook's sketch of the shingler, whose identity is partially concealed by the face guard. His stance is of one who is resigned to his fate, perhaps even dejected by having to work in iron boots - and who wouldn't be? So, this is art that rejects a romanticising view of industrial work and instead asks us to empathise with the men who find themselves trapped in it. These two images do not reference the power of the workers, but rather the powerlessness of their experience. Contemporary accounts report that work in the factory was physically arduous, if not exhausting. It provided relatively secure employment with a strong sense of camaraderie among the workforce, but there were costs in human terms for those making their livings in this fashion.

In a related 1944 image The Drop Hammer, Cook shows a figure brushing scale from white-hot metal with a 'whisk' made of hazel branches.

This kept the surface of the heated metal clear while it was being shaped by hammer blows delivered by hand rather than a steam operated machine. The same low technology work tool appears in a 1942 oil painting by Cole called 'Shaping The Keel of a Corvette', which is in the Laing Gallery in Newcastle upon Tyne. Such was the daily routine for the worker charged with being in close proximity to life-threatening danger and armed only with a primitive brush.

That there were risks to be taken at work in hazardous conditions, sometimes with fatal consequences, is a theme returned to several times by Alfred Williams. His description of the dangers of using a special wheelbarrow to move white-hot metal across the factory floor is particularly disturbing. His account was published in 1915, but this life-threatening practice continued at least until the outbreak of WW2. Williams writes,

> Accidents are frequent at the rolling mills. Burns are of common occurrence, and they are sometimes very serious and occasionally fatal. Great care is requisite in moving about amid so much fire and heated material, for everything - the floors, principals, rollers, the bogie handles, tools and all - is very hot. Some of the carrying is done with a kind of wheel-barrow that requires a special balance. The least obstruction will upset it, and a little awkwardness on the part of the workman is sufficient to bring the weltering burden down to the ground.'
> Williams, 1915)

Williams went on to describe an accident in which a young man died as a result of the wheelbarrow's load falling on him. Because it had only two wheels, this device was hard to manoeuvre in close quarters and so workers resorted to pushing it also with their feet to maintain control. Hubert Cook's oil painting about this subject is from 1943, but it is effective in capturing the physical effort and the risk to life and limb involved. It is one of the few pictures he made in a more impressionistic style with a colour pallet designed to heighten the sense of heat and bright light. The man has his back to the viewer and his elongated limbs emphasise the movement and physical effort demanded of him when so close to the source of intense heat and light.

In the same period as Cook's painting, women were being recruited to the GWR factory to replace men serving in the armed forces. A propaganda film made to promote their contribution to the home war effort also incidentally shows the same wheelbarrow in use. Cook's painting might be criticised for lacking objectivity on the grounds of artistic licence. However, the film makes it abundantly clear that this means of transporting heated materials at high risk had not gone out of use since Williams described it nearly three decades

THE WORKER AS ARTIST

*Railway Works Interior by Hubert Cook 1943. Oil on canvas. 56 x 46cm.
Courtesy of Museum and Art Swindon. AG2009/3*

earlier. A still photograph from the black and white film confirms the accuracy both of Cook's painting and of Williams' first hand written account. To the right of the image is a woman worker who is again holding a hazel brush and operating a lever that provides access to the forge. To the left a workman is indeed dangerously manoeuvring a wheelbarrow laden with white-hot metal with his right foot.

The 'shingler' at work in the GWR factory, watched by a woman with a hazel brush. From a GWR promotional film during WWII

Interpreting the impact of these images means taking account of their independent agency. Teamwork and collectivism counterposed with individual sacrifice may have been the metaphors intended by artists. But, they are out of step with the health and safety at work protocols enjoyed in modern post industrial society. In addition to describing a lost way of work in a documentary sense, the art is also radical in asking the viewer to imagine the heat, smells, sounds and touch of the foundry. However, contemporary and modern audiences have different historical frames of reference. So, the meaning given to these images by today's audiences reflects how attitudes and practices have changed in the century since Cole and Cook began their artistic journeys.

Both Cole and Cook worked in lithography during their time in Swindon and some of their work survives both from the ESU exhibitions and where it was later sold. A copy of Cole's 1938 lithographic print 'Girl Undressing' was bought by the British Council. Cole used this printing technique again in his 1936 depiction of 'A Seated Blind Woman', believed to be of his grandmother. A drawing with a similar subject 'Portrait of an Old Lady' won a silver medal at the 1932 GWR exhibition. Cole uses the contrasts between light and dark to particularly dramatic effect. However, this is more than a straightforward and expert image of an elderly woman. She is dressed in her finery with folded hands and her dignified posture suggest a restful person. But, all of this is unseen by her and the light in which it is depicted is all the more poignant emanating as it does from behind her eyes. This is an image of living with disability, a personal experience that only the visually impaired can understand and that her artist grandson witnesses. It succeeds in narrowing the emotional distance between subject and viewer and is an early pointer to Cole's empathy with the lives of his subjects.

Cole's compassionate interest in the lives of his subjects is also apparent in his Shove Halfpenny about a pub board game often played for money. This print on paper was made in 1938 and is in the Museum and Art Swindon collection. The archive there also has the original proof lithograph made six years earlier when the artist was 22 years old. Light shines from the board to illuminate the two central characters whose exaggerated rounded shapes show the intensity of their competitive playing. Their attention and ours is drawn to the gaming board until the line of shoulders rising from left to right culminates in the stout waistcoated figure behind them. This is an effective device to link both front and rear picture planes, with the action between the two main figures as clear as the third man's intentions are unspoken. The contrast here is between certainty and doubt, perhaps the central contradictory emotions of the gambler. The elements of social commentary in this image point to Cole's awareness of the accepted role of drink and gambling in working class life, but also hint at their potential toxicity.

Blind Woman by Leslie Cole 1936. Lithographic print. 55 x 88cm. Courtesy of Museum and Art Swindon. SWIMG:AG20

Cole made two oil paintings of scenes inside a local pub. The location is not specific, but his

Shove Halfpenny by Leslie Cole 1936. Proof Lithograph. Museum and Art Swindon. SWIMG:AG17

attention to the subject is insightful and endearing. There is a reference here to a famous 1882 painting by Eduard Manet of the Bar at the Folies Bergère in Paris. Cole would have known about this provocative picture from his art studies. Like Manet's, his version is strong on realism - but the contrast with a bourgeois evening of top hats and champagne in Paris could not have been greater. The sexual overtones of Manet's painting are missing and the bar is populated not by the rich, but by serious working-class beer drinkers who always have a grip on their pint pots. In Manet's painting the barmaid may be a product for sale as much as the drinks she has on offer. However, Cole's well-dressed landlady and her customers enjoy a different relationship. She is the dominant, upright figure and is juxtaposed with the pub drinkers who are older men. By comparison with her, they are all plainly dressed and seem shrunken by their daily toil in working-class jobs.

Cook made numerous images of the nature of this working life in the GWR factory. The original drawing he made of men unloading a railway waggon is in the Science Museum. It was used as a proof for six prints and won the bronze medal for lithography at the 1959 Paris salon. In addition to the print in Swindon, another is in the collection of the Metropolitan Museum in New York. This image cleverly anticipates the physical effort of manual

Pub Scene by Leslie Cole. c.1930s. Oil on paper. Private Collection

labouring: the men crouch and lean forward, ready to lift and carry together. They are individuals, but work together in a collective. This is neither glamorous nor romanticised work, but we can see that their concentration and teamwork are needed in demanding physical conditions. Giant machinery and buildings dominate a dark and oppressive background. However, all of the light in the picture is on the three men to emphasise their experience of manual work. Like much of Cook's successful industrial art, this image challenges us to empathise with the dignity of the common labourer.

Another of Cook's lithograph prints of men at work is his 1937 Hydraulic Riveters. This shows men working at a round shaped brazier in the foreground. From here hot metal pieces are passed to the riveter above for fixing in iron plates that were being joined together. The hydraulic cable snakes from the riveter's left, but he has his back to the viewer and the detail of his actions cannot be seen. This concealment has the effect of retaining attention on the two figures at the base of a conventional triangular composition. We are not asked to appreciate the skill of the riveter, but rather the work of these lesser figures who are physically and hierarchically below the status of the riveter. The importance of hierarchy in the GWR Works, as often in social life outside, is designated by head wear. Workers could only don flat caps, but foremen were distinguished by their bowlers and overseers and managers

Unloading at a Railway Siding by Hubert Cook 1953. Original ink drawing on paper for a lithograph. 26 x 21cm. Courtesy of Museum and Art Swindon

by homburgs and trilbies. There were harsh penalties for anyone abusing this hierarchy. The topmost figure in this scene supervises the riveting in a stylish outfit by comparison with the others, but none of the workers is equipped with any discernible safety clothing. Rolled up shirt sleeves indicate a relaxed and perhaps complacent approach to the risks of accidents in close proximity to heat and noise. There is no attempt by Cook to romanticise masculinity in this work setting that is dark, yet illuminated by heat. The male figures' naturalistic rounded shapes clash sharply with the angular materiality of their surroundings, reinforcing human fragility in extreme working conditions.

Hydraulic Riveters by Hubert Cook, 1937. Lithographic print on paper. Author's copy

Electric Welder by Hubert Cook 1938. Lithographic print. 57 x 45cm. Courtesy of Museum and Art Swindon SWIMG:2016.56.21R

Normal though those conditions may be for the worker, the effect of Cook's treatment of the subject is to endorse our empathy with them.

The subject of welders was tackled repeatedly in the art made at Swindon in the inter-war years. The bright light depicted in the picture proved as inspirational then as it had done for medieval religious artists attempting to visualise the divine light of the deity. For the industrial artist the technical challenge was to capture the moment when the sparks fly from the welder's flaming gun. Without it, the moment of contrast with rest of the scene would be lost. Cook made a lithograph of this in 1938, a print of which was bought by the War Artist's Advisory Committee after being exhibited at the Royal Academy in that year. However, even this did not convince the authorities that he should have a commission as a war artist. He followed this with a 1943 version in oil on canvas and these two images bear comparison.

Both images use light and dark to suggest form and depth, with the worker brought to the fore against a darkened background. They are similar in figurative composition, but the detailed lithograph gives a fuller account of the factory setting with equipment and goods throughout. Concentration and effort are stressed, so these images are about the combined mental and physical energy of labour. Electric arc welding can produce sparks and burning and set clothes on fire. A welding helmet and protective suit made from asbestos

Electric Welder by Hubert Cook 1943. Oil on canvas. 75 x 50cm. Courtesy of Museum and Art Swindon AG99

- now known to be an extreme health hazard in its own right as the cause of mesothelioma - were then sole protection to avoid the risks of injury.

By contrast with the lithograph, the worker is the sole focus of the painting. This is an example of Cook's substitution of near photographic detailed depictions in the lithograph with an impressionistic approach in the oil painting developed later in his career. Here the worker is presented in the front

The Toilers by Hubert Cook 1965. Oil on canvas. 58 x 43cm. Courtesy of Museum and Art Swindon AG2009/4.

picture plane at the expense of a wider context and the slightly exaggerated curves in his lower body shape emphasise a strenuous half-crouched position. The stance with legs apart and the firm grip on the welding rod communicate the man concealed from the viewer by his protective headgear. The effect of this depersonalising is reinforced by a more expressive painting technique with broad brush strokes stressing the asbestos suit which renders him bulky and larger than life. He might be the industrial equivalent of the heroic male figure of mythology who prevails when faced by a hazardous encounter. However, to a modern viewer the painting does more to venerate the worker's endurance of challenging conditions.

The theme of daily labour and a working life in exacting circumstances is one to which Cook returned in The Toilers from 1965. This was at the end of his second career as a further education lecturer and the year before he died, yet he returns to the lasting memories from thirty years earlier of his time in the GWR factory. Here he abandons the professional rigours of order and precision in technical drawing. He had become well known for this specialism and published two books about technical drawing. However, this impressionistic oil painting is less concerned with figurative accuracy and is another assault on the senses about working conditions. Heavily suited in protective clothing, the two figures blend into each other with the body of one expressed in a curve of the other's physical effort. The figures again are impersonal and any attempt to capture facial features is unnecessary in the intensity of the moment. Cook knew these working conditions first-hand, so there is little to suggest he was incorporated into a propagandistic purpose. There are the physical privations of labouring to imagine when viewing his images. Together with this assault on the imagination the taste, sight, smell and sound of heat and burning metal are invoked. The viewer is asked not to celebrate personal sacrifice, but to relate to and empathise with it.

Conclusion

COLE AND COOK'S art is effective in prompting sensory responses: for example, what were the textural and tactile sensations whether protective gear was worn or not in a hothouse atmosphere? How did workers cope with the sounds and smells in a factory handling molten metal and using the deafening force of giant steam hammers? Loss of hearing was considered quite normal in the noisiest parts of the factory, such as the boiler-making shop. The background to these experiences was a management style here found wanting in its care for the safety of the Company's shop floor workforce.

This conclusion is reached solely with the benefit of hindsight and informed by modern health and safety at work regulations in western economies. It is clear from the confirmatory written, artistic and photographic evidence that established practices in metal working had changed little in the course of the first half of the twentieth century. This continuity coincided with the GWR's global engineering prominence and commercial successes which made it hugely profitable to shareholders. So, it is hard to avoid the conclusion that the factory exploited and oppressed its workforce in extreme circumstances.

In these respects, the discussion above confirms that Cole and Cook's images - drawings, paintings and prints - are an important documentary record. There has been a temptation to put their images into this visual category and regard them principally as evidence of a lost industrial past. The case for doing so is all the more powerful given that they personally re-presented what they saw in their daily lives in and out of the GWR Works. Theirs was an art based on experience.

However, the danger in these standpoints is that they lend themselves too readily to a certain kind of official narrative. For example, Cole and Cook's art does not seem to have been seen by contemporaries as anything other than normalising the working conditions in the GWR factory. But, for a full appreciation of the significance of their industrial art we should take different audiences into account. The meaning attached to art can and does vary between audiences over time. In the process, the art becomes instrumental in challenging the official version of the industrial past in relation to the post-industrial present. Cole and Cook's generation could never have anticipated how radical the social consequences would be from post-1945 economic restructuring. Although perhaps never intended as a critical stance about the institutions and processes of social inequality, their art has the potential to prompt a modern audience to respond in exactly those terms. It can speak beyond the straightforward and descriptive interpretations placed on it as a documentary record. It can also provoke critical thinking about the present as much as about the past in a meaningful way.

The artistic endeavours of working class people rarely generated a high profile outside of the realms of artisanal craft. From Britain's industrialisation in the mid-18th century through to the de-industrialisation of the late 20th century, this experience based people's art has been largely ignored. And yet, despite the substantial obstacles in their way, many workers used what little time they had outside of the grind of factory life to engage in creative activities. They were inspired with little by the way of formal education to draw, paint, sculpt, write and so on.

For its part, the academic discipline of Art History has recently become more inclusive. This is typically linked to the pivotal essay by Linda Nochlin in 1971, 'Why have there been no great women artists?'. Many feminist authors have since continued to challenge the historical bias inherent in art made by men, curated by men and bought and sold by men. The well established traditions in the creative and commercial aspects of art have been opened up in other ways as well over recent decades, notably through gender-neutral, post-colonial and queer critiques. The breaking down of formal barriers to art is also expressed through the rise of conceptual and installation art, and the challenging notion that art can be transitory as much as fixed. While social class may be a common factor running through these movements for change in art and art history, there is little prominence given to the art of the industrial working classes in their own right. This chapter is a contribution to this field and an attempt to reset the balance.

References

Baxandall, Michael 1988. *Painting and Experience in Fifteenth Century Italy* (Oxford University Press)
Feaver, William 1993. *Pitmen Painters: the Ashington group 1934-1984* (Carcanet Press)
GWR Magazine 1929, 193-195
GWR Magazine 1935, 663
Manifesto 1926. To All Employees of the Great Western Railway. Swindon Central Library Local Studies Collection: SWI 702
Yorke, Malcolm 2010. *The Artistry of Leslie Cole: today I worked well - the picture fell off the brush* (Fleece Press).

8
THE MAKING OF HERITAGE IN SWINDON
BY PHILIP GARRAHAN

Introduction

THIS BOOK BEGAN by highlighting the distinction between the manufacture of trains and the people who made them. The aim has been to put right some of the imbalances both in the literature and in a wider understanding about Swindon. It does this by bringing original social research and writing about a company town into a single volume. This is not without its pitfalls, since there are many areas that have not been covered. For example, the astonishing size and longevity of the workers' library in the Mechanics' Institute (MI) is just one of the many innovations in the town justifying much further study. It amply served its purpose from 1841 until the first municipal library in Swindon was opened in 1943. Other topics might be how religion and temperance movements influenced social allegiances and practices in the town, the role of trade unions in and outside of the GWR Works, or the political outcomes of local and parliamentary elections. The writers of this book will feel they have succeeded if subsequent interest is heightened in topics about this broader history of Swindon's industrial life.

In the meantime, there is the not inconsiderable matter of making connections with the past to memorialise historical change and events. In the first quarter of this century, Swindon has seen a revived interest in its history as a railway town - not least with the opening of the Steam Museum (TSM) in 2000. Since then, several local policy initiatives have sought to bring the town's heritage to the fore. It is apt, therefore, that this concluding discussion takes a forward look based on the historical research. It assesses the heritage sector in Swindon, with specific reference to the redevelopment of the GWR Works and the role of nostalgia in celebration of the town's railway history. Heritage is what we make of the past today with an eye on how this will be remembered in the future. Heritage is in effect the result of interventions and interactions between many different bodies with a public, and often a commercial interest. In this context, therefore, heritage is not a given but a social construct with multiple public and private agencies involved.

The heritage sector is as much about the present as about how Swindon's heritage will be preserved for future generations. A critical issue in heritage policies is how to go about this and there is commonly a resort to nostalgia as a means of doing so. The argument to follow is that policies evoking emotions such as nostalgia have had negative as well positive connotations, with shifts in the way these are managed to suit different economic and political purposes. Today, established heritage perspectives rely on positive feelings about the past and this shift in the management of emotional responses needs to be addressed. When Swindon's locomotive engineering factory closed in the 1980s, the dominant emotions were negative as the social crisis caused by redundancies unfolded. This was entirely typical in the political environment of the time. Government de-industrialisation policies were influenced by neoliberal economic ideas. These ideas initially were expounded by an American economist, Milton Friedman, and found favour on the right of the political spectrum. They were most prominently embraced by Ronald Reagan's Republican government in the USA and Margaret Thatcher's Conservative government in the UK. Both leaders pursued an agenda that aligned with the operation of free markets at the expense of state interventions. So, neoliberalism can be summarised as serving a free enterprise economy, the removal of state regulations, the sale of publicly owned industries and minimising the tax burden on companies and individuals.

There are some aspects of working for the Swindon GWR which are known, but rarely highlighted or theorised together. For example, GWR apprentices in Swindon were referred to locally as 'doing time Inside', a metaphor intended to capture the significance of initial, practical training in the train manufacturing industry. However, this also conveyed the sense of giving something up from an individual identity in order to walk through the factory gates every day. Neither were whole families immune to the influence of the GWR in their homes. The sons of existing employees were preferred for apprenticeships alongside their fathers in specific workshops. This kept the best-paid jobs in the family, while also transferring the burden of managing the apprentice's behaviour to the father. Such contractual conditions in getting employment in the best jobs were ambivalent. As a result, they acted as both a benefit and a burden to wage earners in the factory. Once apprenticed, employees were managed by a severe factory discipline in keeping to the clock. There were rules to be followed about timekeeping which came with strong penalties for any deviation. In addition, hierarchies of control and management extended to headgear worn in the Works. Common labourers were only allowed to wear flat caps, since under-foremen were identified by their trilbies, foremen by bowlers and managers by homburgs. Any departure from this sartorial social order was met with harsh sanctions. Discipline in the workplace, and by extension in the community surrounding the Works, enabled corporate social control in an industrial society.

These and many other GWR management practices pose critical questions for understanding working life in the GWR factory during the period covered by this book. Many improvements to working conditions happened during the course of the century after the 1840s - not least because trade unions were decriminalised and became counterweights to imperious company disciplines. Nevertheless, as the last chapter has demonstrated, at the outbreak of WWII some working practices remained unchanged from the nineteenth century.

Closure and Revivalism

THE RAILWAY WORKS in Swindon closed in 1986 under the neoliberal economic ideology which initially was embraced by Conservative governments, but largely continued under a cross-party consensus. This marked the end of the post-1945 social contract that protected the welfare state in a mixed economy of private and public ownership. The Thatcher and Major governments in particular turned away from old, unionised and state supported industries. Sectors such as mining, shipbuilding and heavy engineering were held to be too dependent on levels of state support and this public expenditure was denigrated for crowding private investment out of the market. The neoliberal notion of rolling back the frontiers of the state was meant to cut public spending and enhance opportunities for the private sector. The private sector could be taxed less if the subsidies paid to ailing nationalised industries were removed. More private investment in the UK economy would be generated as a result. These contentions were inspired by an ideological commitment to the power of markets as the driving force for economic growth and stability, a theory that has been devastated by financial and economic crises in the twenty-first century.

Manufacturing was a major casualty as the UK transitioned into a post-industrial state. It was reduced to a minor role in the overall economy and its place was taken by other sectors, notably finance and services. Amongst these tumultuous changes there was no place for a positive response like nostalgia.

All of the official government messaging marched under the neoliberal banner. There was 'no alternative' to government policy and dissenters were sidelined as 'moaning Minnies'. Both phrases came from the Prime Minister, Mrs Thatcher, who famously avoided travel by train. The far-reaching industrial closures of the time were not heralded with nostalgia about the past, but with its opposite - nostophobia, or an aversion to or fear of returning to it. Old state-dependent, unionised industries were to be thought of only as contributing to the country's misfortunes. Of course, this was of little comfort to the thousands who lost their jobs and their enduring community memories. Celebrations of the age of steam in Swindon would have to await for another day, when they could be managed by a more positive emotional agenda.

The remaking of economic and social landscapes since the 1980s has been extensive in many former industrial towns in the UK. De-industrialisation did not entirely destroy Swindon's industrial architecture to the extent observed by urban geographers in other manufacturing areas. (DeSilvey and Edensor) The rapid demise of heavy industrial sectors had dramatic visual effects on the industrial landscapes of many regions in the UK. Pit-head winding gear, shipbuilding yards, steel works and coking plants have all but disappeared where once they were a common sight. In an extreme case, the north east of England is said to retain more evidence of the Roman occupation than of its recent industrial past. The radical removal of industry-related architecture was followed by economic regeneration policies based on encouraging foreign inward investment, which has met with mixed results. However, a common feature throughout the country today is the part played by the heritage sector acting as a conduit for revivalist strategies following de-industrialisation.

Swindon's history as a former railway town differed by virtue of the post-1945 diversification of its local economy along the M4 corridor. By contrast with closures in extraction or manufacturing sectors, railways have been sustained as an integral piece of modern communications infrastructure. The call to the past in Swindon is, therefore, less acutely felt than in colliery towns, for example, where pit closures have not been followed up with sustainable economic diversification. Yet the emotional pull of railway memories in Swindon is joined by the push from the institutions and policies of its heritage sector. Attendant on this, new venues for consumption and leisure have played an important role in de-industrialisation. The most significant site for these purposes in Swindon was the GWR Works, transformed since closure to serve the transition to post-industrial norms through new ownership and radically changed functions.

Before it closed as the result of neoliberal economic and fiscal policies, the railway factory in Swindon had been in decline for some decades. A process of cleaning up the Works site in preparation for new property development began. This led to many buildings on the site being demolished to make way for new offices and blocks of high-end flats. The claim that this process preserved the more historically significant buildings is contested, yet there is no doubt that the derelict site has been improved by diverse retail, leisure, office and housing uses. Included in these is the large designer outlet shopping centre opened in 1997 by the McArthur Glen company. It is particularly poignant that one of the famous steam engines once made on this site is installed at a main entrance to the shopping centre. Its purpose is to entertain shoppers in an age of possessive individualism and be a compelling reminder of the site's historical significance. This installation is touching because it evokes a keen sense of awareness of Swindon's past by playing on a nostalgic emotional response. It perhaps goes much further than intended, however, critically encapsulating the transition from an age of production to one of consumption. Where once thousands laboured to manufacture trains, now similar numbers fill the avenues of a shopping mall. The upheavals and shockwaves of the national journey from an industrial to a post-industrial economy and society could never have been so radically illustrated in direct material terms.

. *The entrance to the McArthur Glen designer retail centre. Author's photograph.*

The shopping centre follows an international pattern of shops, food courts and giant car parks evoking that 'sameness of place' linked to globalisation and the transition to post-industrialism. There is little internal evidence of the building's origins and previous uses, other than the retained overhead iron beams and lifting gear and a few restored turning machines. Culture rarely intervenes in the commerce transacted between shops and consumers in the mall. However, the mall briefly featured a small exhibition by a local artist who began his career in the railway factory. He dryly noted the significance attached to his work by the outlet centre, when it was hung in the corridor leading from the shops to the public toilets.

Other improvements, to what otherwise might have remained a derelict site, included attracting key national agencies. The National Trust has purpose-built national headquarters on the site and it is joined by Historic England, English Heritage, the National Monuments Records Centre and the UK Space Agency in the surviving Works buildings. There is thus a concentration of public agencies specialising in the preservation of historic places without parallel elsewhere in the UK. The sad irony of their proximity to the semi-derelict Mechanics' Institute (MI) has not been lost on the generations of local campaigners seeking to restore this building by private or public means. At the time of writing, the MI is high on the Victorian Society's list of the country's most endangered historic buildings

The Steam Museum

NOW HOUSED IN large and refurbished GWR workshops to accommodate an extensive collection of railway equipment and memorabilia, TSM is the lead agency based on Swindon's railway heritage. It is not a general purpose museum, but styles itself as The Museum of the Great Western Railway. It is currently part of the local authority's service called Museum and Art Swindon, which also runs the town's newly opened exhibition space in the civic offices, the Lydiard House Museum and the Richard Jefferies House Museum. TSM has an extensive collection and archive and its standing is high in respect to outreach work, especially with schools. In practice, the category of the living museum is distinguished from others by virtue of its invitation to experience the past through the lives of people in history. The experiential benefit hypothetically lies in the extent to which such a museum can recreate the imagined conditions of relevant ways of life. In Swindon's case, the 6,500 square metre TSM was designed as a living museum with an almost £8 million grant from the National Heritage Memorial Lottery Fund.

The museum responds to Swindon's railway heritage through its mission to educate and entertain. It signals its railway history in advance with the promise that visitors will get a 'A First Class day Out'. TSM's account of its mission is instructive: 'Situated right opposite the Swindon Designer Outlet, the museum tells the story of the men and women who built, operated and travelled on the Great Western Railway, often referred to by historians and railway fans as 'God's Wonderful Railway'. (TSM) However, this is a story that is only partially told. It is a redacted account of Swindon's social history that does not fully capture some of the important dimensions of working and social life in a company town. In this respect, there is a case for a critical approach to its claims to authenticity.

TSM acknowledges many of the well documented realities of working for the GWR. For example, the fact that the railway industry was second only to coal mining and shipping for the risk of fatal injury to its workers. This theme of health and safety at work is briefly touched upon by the exhibits, but little mention is made of the pivotal worker-run Medical Fund Society analysed in Chapter 3 above. This is especially significant given the Fund's innovative and long-standing record locally, quite apart from its role in relation to the country's national health policies and the founding of the NHS. Neither is there sufficient attention paid to the housing and public health issues analysed in Chapter 2, or the innovations in adult education at the Mechanics' Institute explained in chapters 4 and 5. There is ample evidence in this book that the boundaries between life and work were blurred by the social order that flourished in Swindon in the age of steam. They made it an exceptional example of a company town and any history of Swindon in the age of steam should attach greater importance to this theme.

Visitors to TSM see short videos from the 1940s which highlight the intense physical labour of individuals and teams in the Works. These echo the interest in these same experiences by local artists analysed in Chapters 6 and 7. However, workers are shown in charge and in defiant and heroic mode. The video films and subsequent exhibits also focus on the limited roles for women workers and in particular their wartime experiences. That there is no hint of class conflict in these dated films is evidently a product of them being made by the GWR as propaganda to promote its corporate image in the most positive light. More recent video film also being shown uses interviews with former GWR employees in Swindon. These feature personal recollections about the sustained camaraderie among members of the workforce and flippant accounts of shop floor nicknames. The thousands of redundancies and community dislocation resulting from the running down of the factory and its eventual closure are given less emphasis.

The displays at TSM often rely on mannequins for visual effects which seem outdated in the digital age. To its credit, these include reference to industrial injuries and to hours and conditions of work. The latter are in a short written account, but almost as marginal notes. The overall impression at TSM derives from the post-industrial assumption of class no longer mattering in the way that it once divided society. The central metaphor makes the point: 'The purchase of the Works site in 1986 by Tarmac Properties offered the opportunity to redevelop a large part of Swindon that was largely unknown to its population. Surrounded by high walls for most of its history, few Swindonians – apart from those who worked there – had much opportunity to view the heritage which had played such an important part in the development of their town.' Bringing down the walls between people that supposedly separated them implies a less divided society, so the land re-use and building conversions were construed as having not just social, but also investor benefits. This ambition is further buttressed by association with protecting the town's industrial legacy: ' What also became apparent was the significance of the architectural heritage, which had survived the 150-year occupation of the site by the GWR and its successors. It was within this context that the building now housing the museum was renovated'. In this way the slate of social class divisions is wiped clean for a new beginning, justified by the universal appeals of heritage and conservation.

The category of the living museum to which TSM belongs largely uses nostalgia to invoke positive memories of a recent past, but such institutions are not without their critics as the terms 'smokestack nostalgia' and 'ruin porn' imply. (Strangleman; Roberts) In general they are accused of pressing social divisions into the background in the cause of highlighting communal harmony. The result is denial about, '…divisions between church and chapel goers and those that attended neither, between 'gaffers' and 'union' men, between respectable and disreputable households.…There was also the corrosive influence of racism and chauvinism…' (Griffin) An early twentieth century critic of the GWR argued that an individual's political views could damage his employment and that, ' …there is no such thing as individual liberty about the Works. He whose opinions are most nearly in agreement with those of the foreman thrives best, obtains the highest piecework prices and the greatest days wages too, while the other is certain to be put under the ban'. (Williams, 191) Putting such features into the margins enables the connotations of social structures and inequalities to be presented descriptively, but without controversy or any connection to today's divided society. That TSM as a living museum is silent on such key dimensions of life in a company town is not to argue it is distorting the past, but potentially of pacifying and de-politicising it. (Spence) The influence of post-industrial regeneration policies can be seen in the dominant lexicon of ideas and language at TSM. Its romanticised view of the GWR's , '…chocolate and cream carriages and copper-capped steam locomotives speeding to the west for holidays by the sea' has attracted specific criticism. This analysis concludes there is, '… no reason to suspect that visitors would be unable to appreciate themes such as trade unionism and militancy, or the massive upheaval caused when British Rail closed Swindon Works in the 1980s'. (Hoadley, 766) Other appeals for TSM to see the bigger picture are made by a labour historian who criticises the museum for trading on the emotive appeal and '…wide-spread popularity of railway history and railway antiquarianism'. This sort of criticism makes a valid point, but should not overlook the very high esteem in which TSM is held both by railway enthusiasts and occasional visitors alike.

In one particular respect TSM shifted the balance slightly by giving new recognition to railway artists. Almost twenty years after opening, it held its first showing of industrial art derived from experience in a public exhibition in the foyer to the museum. This was called The Art of Industry and it involved hosting part of a Swindon Museum initiative, Art on Tour which was begun during the 2020-2021 Covid pandemic lockdowns. Another solo exhibition has restricted public access. It consists of twelve works by Hubert Cook hung in a corridor of TSM offices not routinely open to the public and which therefore are only viewed by appointment. But, such railway-worker, experience-based art is largely absent from TSM's extensive main exhibition halls and this is more poignant in view of its institutional mission. Industrial art may be widely overlooked elsewhere, but this example of a living museum should be encouraged to take a different turn.

The commercial basis of TSM means that it operates under an imperative to maximise attendance numbers and this is driven by making the broadest possible appeal to its market. At the time of writing a day ticket for a family of four costs £43, already putting a visit beyond the reach of lower income groups. Under more relaxed financial strictures a different curation might provoke a modern audience to reflect not just on the past, but also on the relation between work and society today. In the process, the Euro/western-centric nostalgia for the past could be challenged by awareness of 19 century working conditions prevailing in many other parts of the 21 century world. TSM's current engagement with the public is centred on the novelty and wonder of the steam train and all of its endearing qualities. Although there are static displays to take the visitor into the lives of those who made the trains, these have distinct features: they occupy a relatively small space; the optics have fallen behind bolder visual journeys made possible in the digital age; and there is little recognition of working life in a company town, warts and all. For the time being, telling the story of the men and women of the GWR in a fuller and more rounded way seems unlikely. The continuing importance of the railway to national transport policies and the link between corporatism and the welfare state could be a new starting point. This could go beyond the nostalgic response to a sanitised version of the past which depends on wistful emotions. Asking how the past and present actively inform each other potentially engages the visitor more actively than nostalgia implies. An important literature has developed in this respect about the functions of nostalgia both as restorative and reflective: in the former the past is simply the context for universal ideals like the personal sacrifice and collective endeavour of industrial labourers in a railway factory; in the latter the past is deployed to engage with contested ideas and practices of the present. Encouragingly, this theme has recently been taken up in research by a living museum in the north east of England with the aim of, '…rethinking sites of working-class heritage from relatively homogeneous celebratory depictions to stories that situate the classed past in global and colonial contexts'. A heritage site such as TSM has much potential to explore these dimensions through a narrative about industrial life in a company town like Swindon. This is a pointer to how the town's heritage might be made afresh.

Conclusion

THIS CHAPTER INTENTIONALLY avoids the temptation to summarise the content of previous chapters in any great detail. This is too often done to advance the cause of a particular theoretical position over others. The result of such an analysis can be effective, but it typically takes on an abstract or conceptual form inappropriate for this book. The authors of this book chose a more empirically grounded approach which mostly covered the century after steam came to Swindon in 1841. In this final chapter, therefore, the opportunity is taken to situate our individual and collective research findings in modern concerns about the making and role of heritage. This debate needs input from critical friends like the contributors to this book to support the town's heritage and fully to reflect the work and the spirit of the people who made Swindon.

References

DeSilvey, Catlin and Edensor, Tim 2013. 'Reckoning with ruins'. In *Progress in Human Geography*. Vol. 37(4). 465-485. https://www.proquest.com/docview/1399052140/fulltextPDF/3A39B331E9004930PQ/1?accountid=14697

Griffin, Colin 2006. 'Public History Essay: Instead of Manufacturing Goods, We Are Manufacturing Heritage: The National Coal-mining Museum for England.' In *Labour history review*. Vol. 71(3) (Maney Publishing) 289-302. https://web-s-ebscohost-com.libezproxy.open.ac.uk/ehost/pdfviewer/pdfviewer?vid=0&sid=c1c1bd67-9c66-4de2-b4d7-fe6fee2b067d%40redis

Hoadley, Stephen 2001. 'Steam: The Museum of the Great Western Railway, Swindon. In *Technology and Culture*, 42(4), 764–766. http://www.jstor.org/stable/25147806

Roberts, Ian 2007. 'Collective Representations, Divided Memory and Patterns of Paradox: Mining and Shipbuilding'. In Sociological Research Online. Vol.12 (6). http://www.socresonline.org.uk/12/6/6.html

Spence, Jean 2020. 'Miner Artist/Minor Artist? Class, Politics, and the Post-Industrial Consumption of Mining Art'. In *Frontiers in Sociology*. Vol. 5 (Article 62) https://www.frontiersin.org/articles/10.3389/fsoc.2020.00062/full

STEAM. https://www.steam-museum.org.uk/about-us/history-of-steam/

Strangleman, Tim 2013. 'Smokestack nostalgia, "Ruin porn" or working class obituary: the role and meaning of de-industrial representation'. In *International Labor Work. Class History*. Vol.84. 23–37. DOI:10.1017/S0147547913000239

Williams, Alfred 2010. *Life in a Railway Factory* (Amberley)

Delving Deeper

Swindon and the Great Western Railway
This field is dominated by trains and their history in Swindon. Despite the strong emphasis on material manufacturing, some sources also present descriptive evidence about social engineering - without necessarily putting this in a critical context. See for example:
Bateman, Ron 2020, The End of The Line: the last ten years at Swindon Works (History Press);
Cattell, John and Keith Falconer 1995, Swindon: the Legacy of a Railway Town (English Heritage);
Historic England 2017. Mechanics' Institutes: Introduction to Heritage Assets (Historic England);
Jefferies, Richard 1986. Jefferies' land: a history of Swindon and its environs. Ed. G. Toplis (Simpkin & Marshall);
Large, Frederick 1932. A Swindon Retrospect 1855-1930 (The Borough Press);
Matheson Rosa 2016, Swindon Works: The Legend (The History Press); Peck, Alan S. 2009, The Great Western Works at Swindon (Heathfield Railway Publications).
Some primary sources are:
BBC. "The NHS: Born in Swindon." Local History http://www.bbc.co.uk/wiltshire/content/articles/2008/06/27/nhs_swindon_60th_feature.shtml;
Gooch, Daniel 1982. Diaries of Sir Daniel Gooch, Baronet. edited by Theodore Martin (Kegan Paul, Trench, Trübner);
Gooch, Daniel. 'Letters of D Gooch, C A Saunders and member of his family, and F G Saunders 1839-1878', 1008/82, RAIL Collection, The National Archives; MI Report 'Reports and Accounts: Welfare, Great Western Railway Mechanics' Institution Swindon,' 1846-1949, RAIL 1115/15, RAIL Collection, The National Archives.

The New Industrial Towns
Only some of the new centres of industry were set in the mould of a company town like Swindon. There has been widespread research into the social

conditions created by industrialisation and railway towns are particularly intriguing because of the pivotal role played by modern transport. See for example:

Guilcher, G. Railway Mania and Press Mania in 1844-45. Cahiers Victoriens & édouardiens, 55 (2002) 81-94;

Matthew, Colin 2005 ed.The Nineteenth Century (Oxford University Press; McLeod, Hugh 1984. Religion and the Working Class in Nineteenth-Century Britain (MacMillan);

Marx, Karl 1975. Wage-Labour and Capital & Value, Price and Profit (International Publishers);

Smith, Adam 1977 The Wealth of Nations, ed. Edwin Cannan (Chicago University Press)

The Railway Village

The Swindon Railway Village is comparable with late 19th century model industrial villages, which it preceded by some decades. The literature about model industrial villages is broad but shallow with Gillian Darley's 2007 Villages of Vision (Five Leaves Publications) and Thomas Markus' 1993 Buildings and Power (Routledge) being amongst the most interesting and comprehensive. For a broader picture see:

Foucault, Michel 2008, The Birth of Biopolitics: lectures at the Collège de France, 1978-79 (Palgrave Macmillan);

Hayden, Dolores 1976 Seven American Utopias: The Architecture of Communitarian Socialism, 1790-1975 (MIT Press);

Radcliffe, Christopher 1997, 'Mutual improvement societies and the forging of working-class political consciousness in nineteenth century England'. International Journal of Lifelong Education 16, no. 2;

Rule, John 1986, The Labouring Classes in Early Industrial England, 1750-1850 (Routledge);

The Builder 1854 A Visit to Swindon New Town The Builder 12, no. 591 289-290;

UNESCO 2021, Saltaire World Heritage List, https://whc.unesco.org/en/list/1028/

The GWR Medical FundSociety

Salubritas et Industria (Well-being and Work) became part of Swindon's coat of arms in 1901. Progressive health insurance and diligent collectivism underpinned Swindon's advanced health and well-being provision. Although this local history has been neglected, it is well served by studies of mutual aid across Victorian Britain. For example:

Cannadine, D. 1998 Class in Britain (Yale);

Daunton, M., 'Risk, redistribution and social welfare in Britain from the poor law to Beveridge' in M. Daunton 1996 (ed), Charity, self-interest and welfare in the English Past (Routledge), pp. 1-22;

Drummond, D.K. 1995 Crewe: Railway Town, Company and People 1840-1914 (Aldershot);

Gosden, P. 1961 The Friendly Societies in England, 1815–1875 (Manchester);

Hardy, A. 2001. Health and Medicine in Britain since 1860 (Rede Globe Press);

Harris, Bernard, The Origins of the British Welfare State: Society, State and Social Welfare in England and Wales, 1800-1945 (Palgrave);

Kidd, Alan 1999 Society and the poor in Nineteenth century England (Palgrave);

Johnson, P. 1996 Risk, Redistribution and Social Welfare in Britain from the Poor Law to Beveridge in Martin Daunton (ed), Charity, Self-Interest and Welfare in the English Past (Routledge);

Neave, David 1991 Mutual Aid in the Victorian Countryside: Friendly Societies in the Rural East Riding 1830-1914 (Hull University Press); Waddington, K., 2007. 'Health and Medicine' in C. Williams (ed), A Companion to Nineteenth century Britain (Wiley), pp. 412-29

Art and Culture in Swindon

This is a very neglected field. There are no published accounts of the lives of Hubert Cook or Harold Dearden. The only full biography of Leslie Cole is by Malcolm Yorke 2010, The Artistry of Leslie Cole (Fleece Press). For a selection of current artworks held by Museum and Art Swindon, see ArtUk: https://artuk.org/discover/artworks/search/2024--keyword:swindon--referrer:global-search-412606/page/2

A 1991 catalogue is published as The Swindon Collection of Twentieth Century British Art (Thamesdown Borough Council). See also;

MacDonald, Stuart, 2005, A Century of Art and Design Education – From Arts and Crafts to Conceptual Art (Lutterworth Press);

Jolliffe, Harold, 1968, Arts Centre Adventure, Swindon Borough Council. (Simpsons Printers);

Carline, Richard, 1968, Draw They Must – A history of teaching and examining of Art (Edward Arnold).

Leonard Clark's Alfred Williams: His Life and Work remains the only full biography of Williams (first published in 1945 by William George's Sons

Ltd [sic], republished in 1969 by David & Charles (Publishers) Limited of Newton Abbot).

However, an unpublished memoir about his life, by his friend, Henry Byett, is part of the Swindon Collection at Swindon Central Library. That archive also contains more information about his life, and editions of all of his published works. The Wiltshire & Swindon History Centre at Chippenham holds a major archive of items associated with his life and work, including manuscripts of both published and unpublished poetry and prose, letters, photographs, official documents, and newspaper cuttings. Caroline Ockwell and Graham Carter co-wrote a book based on a chapter from Williams' book, A Wiltshire Village, in 2012, called The Shadow of the Workhouse. Williams' major contribution to the preservation of English folk song lyrics features on the official website of the English Folk Dance and Song Society (see https://archives.vwml.org/records/AW).

The Published Works of Alfred Williams
Songs in Wiltshire, 1909 (Erskine Macdonald)
Poems in Wiltshire, 1911 (Erskine Macdonald)
Nature and Other Poems, 1912 (Erskine Macdonald)
A Wiltshire Village, 1912 (Duckworth & Co Ltd)
Cor Cordium, 1913 (Erskine Macdonald)
Villages of the White Horse, 1913 (Duckworth & Co Ltd)
Life in a Railway Factory, 1915 (Duckworth & Co Ltd)
War Sonnets and Songs, 1915 (Erskine Macdonald)
Round About the Upper Thames, 1922 (Duckworth & Co Ltd)
Folk Songs of the Upper Thames, 1923 (Duckworth & Co Ltd)
Selected Poems, 1925 (Erskine Macdonald)
Tales from the Panchatantra, 1930 (Basil Blackwell) republished as Tales from the East, 1931 (Basil Blackwell)

Understanding Heritage
Much has been written about the Heritage sector in recent years and a good source of the many different perspectives is Fairclough, Graham et.al. (ed.) 2008, The Heritage Reader (Routledge). The definitive account of authorised heritage discourse is in Smith, Laurajane 2006, Uses of Heritage (Routledge). For a background on debates about community and identity, see Anderson, Benedict 1983, Imagined Communities (Verso).

INDEX

This is primarily an index of people and places, although some themes and institutions are also included.

Ablett, Thomas 110
Addison, Christopher 48
Aire, River 30
Anderson, E E 103, 104
Apsley House 114
Armstrong, Joseph 40, 62, 65, 88
art 3, 7, 71, 85, 117–43, 153; see also Art, School of
Art, School of 5,7, 93–115
Ashington (Northumberland) 125
Ashton, Frederick 67
Atkinson, Anglea 43
Attlee, Clement 49
Attwood, Harry Carleton 105, 107
Austen, Jane 19

Bailey, G A 122
banking, banks 12, 68
Bath 10, 41, 65, 100, 109
   Road 114
stone 27, 53
Bathampton Street 15, 16, 19
baths, Turkish 20, 24, 37, 41, 61
Belsen, Bergen-, camp 124
Bentham, Jeremy 94
Bergen-Belsen camp 124
Berry, T Percival 40
Betjeman, John 6, 54
Bevan, Aneurin 24, 36, 37, 49–51
Beveridge, William 37, 48, 49
Bickham, W E 107
Binyon, Brightwen 58, 99
Birkbeck, George 28, 30, 97
Birmingham 119, 122
Blackwell, Basil 72
Blaise Castle and Hamlet 19

Bolton 10
Borodin, Alexander 66, 67
Bradford (W Yorks) 10, 30
Bristol 1, 4, 9, 10, 14, 15, 41, 97, 109
   Street 19
Bromborough Pool 10, 30
Brown, J E C 122
Brunel, Isambard K 4, 6, 9, 10, 12–15, 19, 21, 31, 32, 56
Brunger, George 40, 46, 49, 50
Brunwin, Donald 55
Busby, Adam 6, 23, 33

Cadbury family 4
Canada 44, 95, 96
Carfax Street 65
Carter, Graham 7, 71, 126
chapels 9, 13, 29, 152
Cheltenham 10
   Street 65
Chester Street 22
Chesterton, G K 50
churches 9, 13, 29, 152
Churchill, Viscount 122
Churchill, Winston 48
Churchward, George J 40, 44, 63
Clark, Leonard 75, 88, 89
Clarke, William 43
Cobham, Viscount 100
Cockbill, Trevor 26, 53–5, 59–62, 65, 68, 99
Cole, Sir Henry 95, 96, 102
Cole, Leslie 7, 71, 107, 118–27, 129, 130, 132–35, 141–42
Coleview Community Centre 60
Collett, Charles B 40, 63
Conservatism 12, 13, 18–19, 30, 49, 62,

146–7
Cook, Hubert 7, 71, 107, 118–26, 128, 129–31, 132, 134—42, 153
Cornwall 59, 122
cottages 11, 14–21, 27, 31, 38
Crewe 4, 10, 37, 44
Cricklade 13

dancing 3, 29, 55–6, 66, 83
Darwin, Bernard 34, 50–1
Darwin, Charles 34
Dawson, Bertrand 48
Dean, William 40, 63
Dearden, Harold 5, 7, 71, 93, 104–15, 118, 119, 124
Derain, Andre 120
Derby 10
Devon 19, 59
Dickens, Charles 75
dispensary 9, 20, 22–4, 31, 37, 42, 47
Dobson, William 120
Down Ampney 67
drawing 25, 97–104, 107, 110, 113, 120–3, 141
Dundee 98
Dyer, – 65

East India Company 122
education 11, 20, 26–30, 47, 61–4, 77–8, 86, 93, 97–105, 117, 141–2, 151
Eliot, George 51
Emlyn, Viscount 58
Emlyn Square 59
Epstein, Jacob 120
Eurich, Richard 120
Evelyn Community Centre 33, 35

Fairclough, Harry Stanley 66–8
Faringdon Street (Road) 17, 19, 22
Farlie, Robert 63
Fauré, Gabriel 68
Fitzmaurice, Lord 101
foremen 76, 80–1, 88, 135, 147,152
Foyles Bookshop 111
Friedman, Milton 146

Gibson, A 40
Glasgow 28
Gloucester Street 65
Gloucestershire College of Art and Design 104

Gooch, Daniel 10, 12–14, 18, 19, 21, 24, 27, 30, 35, 36, 40, 41, 56, 59, 62, 63, 65, 66, 68, 98
Granados, Enrique 68
Greece 124
Greek 6, 81
Gresley, Nigel 63
Guy's Hospital 41

Halifax 104
Harford, John 19
Hawksworth, Frederick W 40, 63
Health Hydro 30, 33, 34
health, public 3, 21, 35–8, 41, 43, 59–60, 64–5, 117, 118, 132, 142, 151
heritage 5, 54–5, 60, 64, 79, 118, 145–54,
Herschell, Lord 101
Hole, James 18
Horner, C E 103
hospitals 9, 20–4, 31, 33, 35, 37, 41–2, 47–50, 65, 79, 108
housing 4–5, 7, 10,14–18, 20, 44, 60, 64–5, 87, 117, 149, 151
Hull 119, 124
Hydro, Health 30, 33, 34

India 72
insurance 38, 45, 48–51
Ipswich 58
Ireland 122

Japan 124
Jefferies, Richard 13, 14, 64, 74, 77–80, 82, 88, 89, 150
Jolliffe, Harold 109
Jowett, Percy 122

Kensington 62, 95, 102, 115

Laing Gallery 130
Lambert, Constant 44, 67
Large, Frederick 14
Lawrence, Ranald 100
Leeds 97
Leicester Galleries 125
Letchworth Garden City 30
Lewis, Harry 5
libraries 3, 24, 26, 28, 30, 53, 55, 58–60, 64, 77, 78, 97, 98, 108, 145

INDEX

Liddington Hill 85
Life in a Railway Factory 6–7, 64, 73–6, 80–1, 84–5, 89, 91
Lindley, Kenneth 114
Liverpool 11, 97, 98
Llynvi and Ogmore Railway 41
Locarno 112
Lockyer, J E 122
Long, Meesrs 100
Lovett, William 96
Lowe, E 122
Lowe, John 40
Lydiard House Museum 150
Lyon, Rolbert 125

McArthur Glen Outlet 149
Malta 124
Manchester 11, 97
Manet, Eduard 134
market 9, 24, 27, 30, 53, 56–8, 99
Marlborough 4
Marx, Karl 17
Massenet, Jules 67
Matisse, Henri 120
Mawson, Clarence 102
Mayne, W Boxer 40
Mechanics Institute 5, 6, 9, 13, 24–31, 35, 37, 41, 42, 51, 53–69, 71, 76–9, 82, 89, 91, 93, 105, 145, 150, 151
Medical Fund Society 3, 5, 6, 13, 20–4, 33–52, 59, 65, 71, 76, 79, 91, 151
Mendelssohn, Felix 61
Merthyr Tydfil 30
Merton Street 65
Messenger, Thomas 43
Methuen, Lord 56, 98
Metropolitan Museum of Art, New York 120, 134
Mexico City 63
Midland Railway 10
Milton Keynes 18
Milton Road 22, 33, 34, 50
Morris, William 40, 64
Moscow 63
Museum, Steam 145, 150–4
music 3, 66–7, 83, 114

Nash, John 19
National Health Service 24, 33, 48–9, 66
Newcastle 130

New Lanark 28
New York 120, 134
Nochlin, Linda 143
North Wiltshire Technical Institute (School) 94, 99–102, 104, 107
Northumberland 14

Ogmore Railway, Llynvi and 41
opera 3, 25, 66–8, 120
Oriel Street 65
Owen, Robert 28, 29
Oxford 72
Oxford Building Society 65
Oxford Street 16, 19,

Paddington 89, 105, 122, 123
Paris 134
Parker, Barry 30, 31
Parkinson, W 102
parks 9, 56, 59
Parry, Martha 55
Patton, J 43
pensions 44, 45
Perkin, Harald 11
Peskett, Z 40
Picasso, Pablo 120
piecework 80, 82–3, 88, 152
Pitmen Painters 118, 125
planning 4, 7, 10, 23, 54–5
Pole, Felix 89
public health 3, 21, 35–8, 41, 43, 59–60, 64–5, 117, 118, 132, 142, 151

Queenstown 65

railway village 9–32
Rea, Minard Christian 40, 65, 68
Reagan, Ronald 146
Regent Street 107, 108
religion 9, 13, 29, 152
Richards, William 65
Rigby, J D and C 15
Rimsky-Korsakov, Nikolai 66
Roberts, Edward 25, 56, 99
Robinson, John G 63
Rochdale 104
Rodbourne Cheney 60
Rolleston, W V 100
Rome 18
Russell, Charles 21

Russia, Russian 24, 63, 66, 67

Sadlers Wells Opera 67
St Petersburg 63
Salford 64
Saltaire 4, 10, 30
Santa Cruz 63
School of Art 5,7, 93–115
schools 3, 30, 42, 47,58, 62, 72, 97, 100, 105, 150
science 12, 30, 59, 77, 99–101
Scotland 15, 94, 96
self-help 12–13, 26, 29, 33, 36–7, 43–4, 51, 55, 61, 96
Senefelder Club 120
Shakespeare, William 75
Sheffield 97
Sheppard, John 15
Shrewsbury 11
Sickert, Walter 120
Silcock, Thomas Ball 100
Simonds, Mr 28
Smiles, Samuel 12, 13
Smith, Adam 11
Smith, John J 22
social engineering 2, 5
South Marston 60, 72, 86, 91
Spencer, F H 64
Spruce, W 40
Stalin, Joseph 129
Stanford, Charles V 67
Stanier, William A 40, 63
Steam Museum 145, 150-4
Stephenson, George 13
Stooke, John 6
Storran Gallery 120
Stratton 60
Stravinsky, Igor 67
Stroud School of Art 99
Sturrock, Archibald 17, 21, 63, 65, 68
Summerhayes, T E 122
Sutton Coldfield 119

swimming baths 3, 9, 20, 22–4, 31, 33–4, 37, 41–2, 47, 50, 51
Swinhoe, G M 40, 65

Taunton Street 16, 19
Tawney, R H 94
technology 12, 41, 74, 97, 130
Tenbury Railway 41
Thatcher, Margaret 146–8
Thomas, W James 122
Toothill 107
Tredegar 36, 42, 51
Treherne, John 64
Turkish baths 20, 24, 37, 41, 61
Turner, J M W 11

United States 95, 146

Vaughan Williams, Ralph 67
Vickers, J S 103
Victoria and Albert Museum 95
Victoria Road 100, 114

Wales, Welsh 9, 14, 37, 48, 118, 122
Wallace, Alfred 107
Wallis, George 95
Walters, S E 40
Wanborough 60
Watcombe estate 19
Watson, – 65
Weston super Mare 59
Weymouth 59
Williams, Alfred 6, 7, 43, 64, 71, 72, 74–91, 122, 126, 130, 131
Willink, Henry 49
Winchester College 103
Wirral 10
Wolverhampton 98
Wroughton 60, 119

York 4, 104

www.ingramcontent.com/pod-product-compliance
Lightning Source LLC
Chambersburg PA
CBHW042138160426
43200CB00020B/2975